SEP 1 6 2015

Eating Disorders

THE STATE OF
MENTAL ILLNESS
AND ITS THERAPY

THE STATE OF
MENTAL ILLNESS
AND ITS THERAPY

Eating Disorders

SHIRLEY BRINKERHOFF

Mason Crest

Mason Crest
450 Parkway Drive, Suite D
Broomall, PA 19008
www.masoncrest.com

Printed in the Hashemite Kingdom of Jordan.

First printing
9 8 7 6 5 4 3 2 1

Series ISBN: 978-1-4222-2819-7
ISBN: 978-1-4222-2825-8
ebook ISBN: 978-1-4222-8986-0

The Library of Congress has cataloged the
    hardcopy format(s) as follows:

        Library of Congress Cataloging-in-Publication Data

Brinkerhoff, Shirley.
    [Drug therapy and eating disorders]
    Eating disorders / Shirley Brinkerhoff.
        pages cm. – (The state of mental illness and its therapy)
    Audience: Age 12.
    Audience: Grade 7 to 8.
    Revision of: Drug therapy and eating disorders. 2004.
    Includes bibliographical references and index.
    ISBN 978-1-4222-2825-8 (hardcover) – ISBN 978-1-4222-2819-7 (series) – ISBN 978-1-4222-8986-0 (ebook) (print)
    1. Eating disorders–Juvenile literature. 2. Eating disorders–Chemotherapy–Juvenile literature. I. Title.
    RC552.E18B75 2014
    616.85'26061–dc23
                        2013008196

Produced by Vestal Creative Services.
www.vestalcreative.com

This book is meant to educate and should not be used as an alternative to appropriate medical care. Its creators have made every effort to ensure that the information presented is accurate—but it is not intended to substitute for the help and services of trained professionals.

Picture credits:
18percentgrey | Dreamstime.com: p. 67. Anita Patterson Peppers | Dreamstime.com: p. 74. Artisticco Llc | Dreamstime.com: p. 102. Artville: pp. 101, 110, 112. Benjamin Stewart: pp. 53, 60, 63. Cheryl Casey | Dreamstime.com: p. 26. Comstock: pp. 12, 56, 73. Corbis: pp. 106, 113, 114. Corel: pp. 20, 23, 25, 29, 30, 31. Daniel Villeneuve | Dreamstime.com: p. 67. Dirk Ercken | Dreamstime.com: p. 19. Konstantin Sutyagin | Dreamstime.com: p. 68. Liz Van Steenburgh | Dreamstime.com: p. 10. Mauricio Jordan De Souza Coelho | Dreamstime.com: p. 105. Monkey Business Images | Dreamstime.com: p. 44. National Library of Medicine: pp. 46, 47, 50, 58. Petar Neychev | Dreamstime.com: p. 95. Photo Disc: pp. 72, 77, 86, 108. Photomax31 | Dreamstime.com: p. 98. Sabphoto | Dreamstime.com: p. 32. Stockbyte: pp. 70. Yuri Arcurs | Dreamstime.com: p. 14. The individuals in these images are models, and the images are for illustrative purposes only. To the best knowledge of the publisher, all other images are in the public domain. If any image has been inadvertently uncredited or miscredited, please notify Vestal Creative Services, Vestal, New York 13850, so that rectification can be made for future printings.

CONTENTS

Introduction
by Mary Ann McDonnell

Teenagers have reason to be interested in psychiatric disorders and their treatment. Friends, family members, and even teens themselves may experience one of these disorders. Using scenarios adolescents will understand, this series explains various psychiatric disorders and the drugs that treat them.

Diagnosis and treatment of psychiatric disorders in children between six and eighteen years old are well studied and documented in the scientific journals. A paper appearing in the *Journal of the American Academy of Child and Adolescent Psychiatry* in 2010 estimated that 49.5 percent of all adolescents aged 13 to 18 were affected by at least one psychiatric disorder. Various other studies have reported similar findings. Needless to say, many children and adolescents are suffering from psychiatric disorders and are in need of treatment.

Many children have more than one psychiatric disorder, which complicates their diagnoses and treatment plans. Psychiatric disorders often occur together. For instance, a person with a sleep disorder may also be depressed; a teenager with attention-deficit/hyperactivity disorder (ADHD) may also have a substance-use disorder. In psychiatry, we call this comorbidity. Much research addressing this issue has led to improved diagnosis and treatment.

The most common child and adolescent psychiatric disorders are anxiety disorders, depressive disorders, and ADHD. Sleep disorders, sexual disorders, eating disorders, substance-abuse disorders, and psychotic disorders are also quite common. This series has volumes that address each of these disorders.

Major depressive disorders have been the most commonly diagnosed mood disorders for children and adolescents. Researchers don't agree as to how common mania and bipolar disorder are in children. Some experts believe that manic episodes in children and adolescents are underdiagnosed. Many times, a mood disturbance may occur with another psychiatric disorder. For instance, children with ADHD may also be depressed. ADHD is just one psychiatric disorder that is a major health concern for children, adolescents, and adults. Studies of ADHD have reported prevalence rates among children that range from two to 12 percent.

Failure to understand or seek treatment for psychiatric disorders puts children and young adults at risk of developing substance-use disorders. For example, recent research indicates that those with ADHD who were treated with medication were 85 percent less likely to develop a substance-use disorder. Results like these emphasize the importance of timely diagnosis and treatment.

Early diagnosis and treatment may prevent these children from developing further psychological problems. Books like those in this series provide important information, a vital first step toward increased awareness of psychological disorders; knowledge and understanding can shed light on even the most difficult subject. These books should never, however, be viewed as a substitute for professional consultation. Psychiatric testing and an evaluation by a licensed professional is recommended to determine the needs of the child or adolescent and to establish an appropriate treatment plan.

Foreword
by Donald Esherick

We live in a society filled with technology—from computers surfing the Internet to automobiles operating on gas and batteries. In the midst of this advanced society, diseases, illnesses, and medical conditions are treated and often cured with the administration of drugs, many of which were unknown thirty years ago. In the United States, we are fortunate to have an agency, the Food and Drug Administration (FDA), which monitors the development of new drugs and then determines whether the new drugs are safe and effective for use in human beings.

When a new drug is developed, a pharmaceutical company usually intends that drug to treat a single disease or family of diseases. The FDA reviews the company's research to determine if the drug is safe for use in the population at large and if it effectively treats the targeted illnesses. When the FDA finds that the drug is safe and effective, it approves the drug for treating that specific disease or condition. This is called the labeled indication.

During the routine use of the drug, the pharmaceutical company and physicians often observe that a drug treats other medical conditions besides what is indicated in the labeling. While the labeling will not include the treatment of the particular condition, a physician can still prescribe the drug to a patient with this disease. This is known as an unlabeled or off-label indication. This series contains information about both the labeled and off-label indications of psychiatric drugs.

I have reviewed the books in this series from the perspective of the pharmaceutical industry and the FDA, specifically focusing on the labeled indications, uses, and known side effects of these drugs. Further information can be found on the FDA's website (www.FDA.gov).

For someone with an eating disorder, each bite may be fraught with anxiety.

Chapter One

The Disorder

Dear Happywithme,

I read some of your posts about anorexia and bulimia on the eating disorders message board last week, the ones where you said you'd be glad to answer people who write to you. You sound like somebody who knows a lot about eating disorders and who might be able to answer some questions I have.

My mother made me go to an appointment with this eating disorders doctor last week. The doctor really made me angry with some of the things she said, like, "You're putting your body in danger by the way you eat!"—that kind of stuff.

Shame and Secrecy

People with eating disorders often feel a sense of shame about their problems—and this shame leads them to secrecy. Although websites provide a "safe," anonymous way of reaching out for help and information, there is no guarantee that the information you find on the Internet is accurate. The fictional character Lindsay ultimately gains a great deal of help from Gina, her Internet friend, but in real life you should always first seek help from a licensed specialist, not random people on a message board. In this case, Gina is a source of support and information for Lindsay—but she might just as easily have been a bogus "expert" who could have led Lindsay in the wrong direction.

She also said she thought I ought to be in their outpatient treatment program. I know that just means they want to make me eat a lot more stuff, and I absolutely refuse to get fat again. I won't do that no matter how hard they push me—I've worked way too hard and too long to get the fat off my body!

Anyway, I don't really have anyone else I can talk to about all of this, and you said in your posts that you'd answer people who wrote to you, so here goes. (I'll try not to ramble on too long, but I have to give you some background so you'll know where I'm coming from.)

My mom started talking to me about being overweight when I was like seven or eight years old, only she called it being "chunky." Back then, she kept warning me not to let myself get heavy or guys wouldn't like me. To tell you the truth, I couldn't have cared less about guys when I was that age, but what she said made me feel different, like maybe I wasn't as good as the other girls my age or something.

Also, I didn't like the look on my mom's face whenever she took me to buy clothes. When I tried on things in the dressing room, she always looked at me like she was sad and disappointed that I was so big. I really wanted to please her, so I quit eating desserts and mashed potatoes and bread—all the stuff I liked best, because she said that stuff would make me fatter. I figured she knew what she was talking about, because she was always on a diet herself.

I tried really hard. Like, when I went trick-or-treating on Halloween, I'd throw away most of my candy—I felt like I'd make my mom upset if I ate it. I don't know whether I actually lost weight or if I just got a lot taller, but for a while my mom quit saying stuff about me being chunky. And the expression on her face when she looked at me was pretty happy, even though I was never what you could really call thin.

Then, when I was eleven, my dad and mom got divorced. That was pretty much the worst thing in my whole life. I remember I cried just about all the time when my dad first left. To make it even worse, when I did get to see him, he usually had one of his girlfriends with him, which made me angry. Most of them were pretty, I guess. And they were all thin, naturally. I remember I always felt big and fat—"chunky"—next to them. My dad and one of his dates would take me out to dinner or to a movie sometimes, but I'd feel embarrassed the whole time, like I was ruining how they looked just by being with them.

When I was nearly twelve, my dad gave me a workout video by this really skinny lady named Jane Fonda. He tried to be real casual about it, like, "Oh, I just happened to pick this up . . . thought you might like to see it . . . blah, blah, blah," but I got the message loud and clear. That's when I really started working on getting thin.

Anyway, this letter is getting way too long, and I don't even know if you'll have time to read it all. So, let me know if you want to write back, okay? If you do, then I'll write you more about what's going on.

Thanks!

Lindsay

P.S. How did you learn so much about eating disorders?

Date: November 12
Subject: RE: Introducing myself
From: <Happywithme@college.edu>
To: Lindsay<lgirl@compnet.com>

Dear Lindsay,

I was glad to get your e-mail, and I'll do my best to answer your questions.

I'll tell you a little bit about myself: I'm no expert on eating disorders, but I had one myself for about six years, from the time I went away to college until I was in my mid-twenties. I had to drop out of college because of it, but I got help, and I've been doing much better for the last two years.

Now I work part-time at an eating disorders center near here, and even though I'm twenty-six, I'm going back to college to study nutrition.

Tell me more about what's on your mind.

Gina (my real name)

Someone with an eating disorder is often constantly preoccupied with both food and losing weight.

Date: November 13
Subject: More about me
From: Lindsay<lgirl@compnet.com>
To: <Happywithme@college.edu>

Hi, Gina.

Thanks for writing me back so fast. And for letting me tell you all this. My mother's pushing me to go back to the doctor again, but I told her there was no way I'd do that! Maybe you can give me some ideas of how to get her off my back.

Anyway, I was telling you how I finally figured out a way to lose the fat. After my dad "just happened" to pick up that exercise video when I was almost twelve, I tried to eat less than I ever had before, and I started exercising a lot. Exercising was just about the only thing I was interested in. I felt kind of down for a couple years after the divorce, and I didn't care about school or sports or anything like that. But I thought he might be happier if I looked better—you know, thinner. So I started exercising and it really helped me. At first I just did aerobics along with that workout video. Then I decided to run, too, in the mornings before school. First I got up half an hour early, then an hour, and went running. My parents were like, "Oh, wow, this is great! You're really taking care of yourself," so I felt good about it, even though I didn't really enjoy getting out of bed at that hour of the morning. But I felt like I was really showing a lot of self-discipline by doing it, and it helped me lose more weight.

By that time, I had the food thing under control, too. An orange for breakfast, no lunch, then a pretty "normal" dinner—that was what worked best for me. Later, besides doing the running and the workout video, I started doing some other exercises in the evening, too, because some days, dinner just made me feel bloated. With the running and the aerobics tape and the exercises I did in the evening, I was exercising maybe two or three hours every day. My friends said they couldn't believe how good I was about sticking with it.

I still wasn't getting thin enough, though. So two years ago, when I was thirteen, I started doing this fasting thing I made up. You don't eat anything but water and diet soda for a whole week, then you eat like usual for the rest of the month. Then you do the fasting week again, and keep doing the whole thing over until you get down to the weight you want. I had to invent all kinds of excuses for why I was doing this, because my Mom got upset when I didn't eat at all.

Then I found this Web site about being pro-ana (that's like being pro-anorexic, but you probably know that already). Readers write in with all these great tips on how to make people think you're eating when you really aren't. I mean, I'm not anorexic or anything, like a lot of them are, but they did have good ideas! So I learned how to fool my mom during that week when I was fasting, and I lost weight pretty quick, but then my mother got on me about losing too much weight. Go figure. I mean, one minute she's giving me all this grief about being "chunky." So I lose weight, and I still can't please her!

Anyway, about a year ago, when I was still fourteen, this weird thing started happening. Everybody started telling me "stop losing weight, you're getting too skinny!" Even my friends. But all I have to do is look in the mirror to see that I'm still totally fat.

So I need help, Gina. How do you get these people to leave you alone? I mean, even my dad is getting into the act now. First he buys me that workout video and tells me I'm looking great when I lose weight, and now he's trying to get me to eat ice cream and cake and stuff. He's even saying things like, "Let's not overdo this diet thing!" Personally, I wish he'd make up his mind.

The way I look at this eating thing is, it's nobody's business but mine what I eat, don't you agree? I'm fifteen now, and I think I can figure out what to feed myself on my own! So what do I tell these people to get them off my back?

More later,
Lindsay

P.S. I was interested to read that you had an eating disorder. That must be a really tough thing to go through!

A person with an eating disorder may feel discouraged because she is never "thin enough."

Psychiatric Disorders

Psychiatric disorders affect the brain and can alter people's thinking, moods, and behaviors. Throughout recorded human history, psychiatric disorders have been described in the writings of many civilizations, including Egypt, Israel, China, India, and Greece. Attempts to remedy these behaviors through the use of both counseling and drugs (often plant products) are also recorded.

Psychiatric disorders include eating disorders such as anorexia nervosa, bulimia nervosa, binge-eating disorders, and other variants of this problem. It is estimated that five million people in America alone are affected by eating disorders every year, and many more millions around the world are also affected.

The two most widely recognized eating disorders are anorexia nervosa and bulimia nervosa. *The Diagnostic and Statistical Manual*, fourth edition, text revision (DSM-IV-TR), the most recent classification of mental disorders by the American Psychiatric Association, includes both of these disorders. The following information is adapted from the DSM-IV-TR.

Anorexia Nervosa

The DSM-IV-TR provides the following guidelines for diagnosing anorexia nervosa:

1. An individual who refuses to maintain her body weight at or above a minimally normal weight for her age and height. The suggested guideline for determining "minimally normal" is 85 percent of the person's expected weight. This weight range is calculated according to Metropolitan Life Insurance tables or pediatric growth charts. Another guideline used requires that the individual have a body mass index (BMI) equal to or below 17.5 kilograms per their height squared (calculated as weight in kilograms divided by height in meters squared). The individual's body build and weight history are always to be taken into consideration in determining the desired weight.

Someone with bulimia may go on eating binges.

2. An individual who has intense fear of gaining weight or becoming fat, even though he is underweight. This concern does not usually lessen when he loses weight. At times, even while he continues to lose weight, his concern over becoming fat continues to increase.

3. An individual who denies the seriousness of her low body weight; who has a disturbance in the way she perceives her weight or shape, or there is an undue influence of body weight or shape on self-evaluation.

4. An individual who misses three consecutive periods (among those who are menstruating).

Anorexia nervosa is divided into two types.

Restricting Type

The individual has not regularly engaged in binge-eating or purging behavior, which includes self-induced vomiting, or misusing laxatives, diuretics, or enemas. This type of anorexia nervosa uses dieting, fasting, and/or excessive exercise to accomplish weight loss.

Binge-Eating Type

The individual has regularly engaged in binge-eating or purging behavior. Purging may include self-induced vomiting, misuse of laxatives, diuretics, or enemas.

Both types of anorexia nervosa are often associated with:

- depressed mood
- social withdrawal
- irritability
- insomnia
- diminished interest in sex

It can be difficult to determine how many of these symptoms are psychological and how many are related to the physical process of starvation or semistarvation.

Obsessive-compulsive features are also often present. For instance, the person may be preoccupied with thoughts of food. She may hoard food, collect recipes compulsively, or engage in rituals that focus on food preparation and eating.

People with anorexia nervosa sometimes have concerns about eating in public. They may also have a strong need to control their environment and be quite inflexible in their thinking. They often are perfectionists, and they may have difficulty express-

diuretics: Drugs or substances that increase the excretion of urine.

enemas: Forcing liquid into the colon through the anus.

ing themselves emotionally.

The semistarvation effects of anorexia nervosa can affect most major organ systems and cause other disturbances. These include:

- leukopenia (decrease of leukocytes, or white blood cells)
- mild anemia
- fatigue, lethargy, and lack of energy
- muscle cramps; wasting away of the muscles
- dizziness, light-headedness, amnesia
- numbness or tingling in the hands or feet
- the cessation (stopping) of menstruation; sometimes, the
- loss of ability to have children
- heart and/or kidney failure
- constipation
- cold intolerance
- lanugo (a fine, downy, body hair on the trunk)
- bradycardia (abnormally slow heartbeat)

Anorexia nervosa seldom begins before puberty, with the typical age of onset between fourteen and eighteen years. A smaller number of cases occur at later ages, but the disorder rarely begins after the age of forty. Males account for only one-tenth of all cases, with 90 percent occurring in females.

Anorexia nervosa happens far more often in industrialized societies where food is plentiful and where attractiveness is linked to thinness. It seems to be most common in the United States, Canada, Europe, Australia, Japan, New Zealand, and South Africa, and it appears to have increased in the last few decades.

anemia: A condition characterized by a reduction of red blood cells, hemoglobin, or blood volume that results in paleness, weakness, and in extreme cases, death.

Some individuals experience only one episode, then go on to recover fully; others struggle with the disease for years and even decades. Of the individuals with this disorder who are admitted to university hospitals for treatment, the long-term mortality rate is 10 to 20 percent. Starvation, suicide, and electrolyte imbalance are the most common causes of death.

Bulimia Nervosa

The DSM-IV-TR provides the following guidelines for diagnosing bulimia nervosa:

1. *Recurring episodes of binge-eating.* Binge-eating is characterized by an individual eating, during a particular period of time, a larger amount of food than most people would eat, given a similar time period and similar circumstances. A food binge also includes the feeling or sense that the individual lacks control over what, or how much, she is eating during the binge episode; in other words, she feels as though she cannot stop.
2. *Recurring inappropriate behavior to prevent weight gain after binge-eating.* This behavior may include self-induced vomiting, the misuse of laxatives, diuretics, enemas, and other medications, excessive exercise.
3. *Both the binge-eating and inappropriate behavior to prevent weight gain occur on the average at least two times per week for three months.*
4. *The individual involved experiences self-evaluation that is unduly influenced by body shape and weight.*
5. *The disturbance does not occur exclusively during episodes of Anorexia Nervosa.*

Bulimia nervosa is divided into two types.

Purging Type

The individual who experiences this form of the disorder regularly engages in self-induced vomiting or misuse of laxatives, diuretics, or enemas.

> **electrolyte**: An ionized salt in blood, tissue fluids, and cells. These salts include potassium and sodium.

Between 70 and 80 percent of individuals who purge after binge eating do so by self-induced vomiting. Vomiting not only relieves the physical discomfort of being so full, it also reduces the fear of gaining weight. Sometimes vomiting becomes a goal in itself, and the individual will make herself vomit after eating either large or small amounts of food. Vomiting can be induced with fingers or instruments, either of which can stimulate the gag reflex. Eventually, individuals find it easy to make themselves vomit, and some can vomit at will.

Others with bulimia (approximately one third) misuse laxatives and diuretics. Only rarely are enemas used as the sole method to purge.

Nonpurging Type

Persons with this form of bulimia do not regularly engage in purging behaviors—instead, they fast or exercise excessively. For instance, the person may go without eating for an entire day—or exercise so much that she no longer has time for other important activities. She may continue to exercise despite injury or medical complications. Bulimia nervosa is associated with:

- symptoms of depression and mood disorders
- anxiety symptoms
- substance abuse or dependence (in at least 30 percent of those with bulimia nervosa), usually involving alcohol or stimulants
- personality disorders, especially borderline personality disorder

Risk Factors for Bulimia

- Being a girl
- Age. Bulimia usually begins in the teens or early twenties.
- Genetics. People with parents or siblings who have bulimia are more likely to develop it themselves.
- Social pressure. Images of idealized body types in the media pressure people, especially women, to be thin.
- Sports. Bulimia is common among gymnasts, runners, wrestlers, and other athletes, who feel pressure to lose weight or limit their eating to get better at their sport.

Adapted from mayoclinic.com/health/bulimia

The effects of bulimia (many due to purging behaviors) include:

- menstrual irregularity
- fluid and electrolyte abnormalities
- metabolic acidosis (increase in acidity of the blood)
- loss of tooth enamel, which leads to chipping of the teeth; the teeth often look ragged or "moth-eaten."
- an increase in dental cavities
- dependence on laxatives, if they are used often

Rare complications include:

- a tear in the esophagus
- a ruptured stomach
- cardiac arrhythmia
- rectal prolapse

When someone has an eating disorder, he may see his normal appetite for food as a form of bondage.

According to the DSM-IV-TR, bulimia nervosa usually begins during late adolescence or early adult life. Like anorexia, it is more prevalent in industrialized countries and among females. Bulimia occurs primarily in Caucasians, though it may also show up in other ethnic groups.

arrhythmia: An irregularity of the heartbeat.

prolapse: The dropping of an organ or other internal part, such as uterus or rectum.

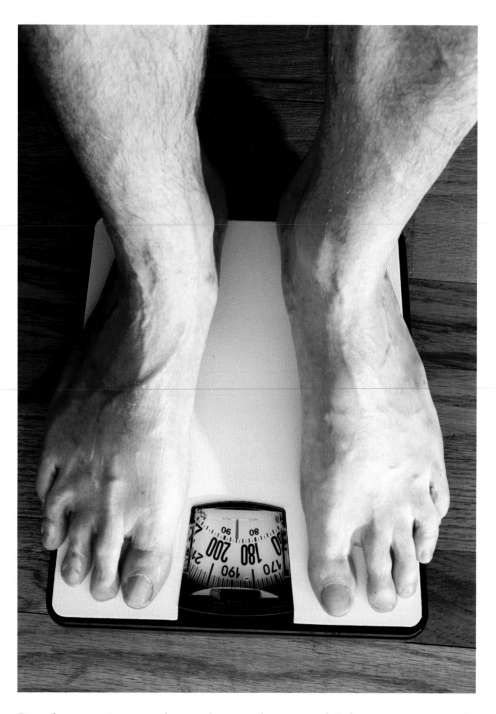

Simply stepping on the scale may be stressful for someone with bulimia.

Eating Disorder Not Otherwise Specified

People sometimes experience eating disorders that do not fit into the criteria for anorexia nervosa or bulimia nervosa. Examples of these types of eating disorders may include variations on anorexia nervosa; for example, the individual's weight may remain within the normal range or she may continue to have regular periods. Other examples include variations on bulimia nervosa, such as the binge-eating happens less than twice a week or for less than three months. In other cases, the individual engages in inappropriate purging behaviors after eating only a small amount of food, or the individual repeatedly chews and spits out—but does not swallow—large amounts of food. Binge-eating disorder includes recurring episodes of binge eating without purging, fasting, or engaging in excessive exercise. The same person may have symptoms of both anorexia and bulimia. Individuals with this type of eating disorder may still be very sick and at risk for many of the complications associated with other eating disorders.

Eating Disorders In History

Eating disorders have a long history—and most of it centers on women—but only in the last century have these disorders become prevalent in North America.

From the thirteenth to the sixteenth centuries, some people, usually women and girls, seemed able to exist without either food or liquid. They were often watched closely by the church, town officials, or neighbors to see if their claims that they ate and drank nothing were true. In many cases, observers could not disprove these claims. The condition came to be known as "anorexia miribilis," a miraculously inspired loss of appetite. Catholicism had a strong influence during this time, and fasting and the control of the appetite were strongly associated with faith, piety, and spiritual beauty. Joan

Jacobs Brumberg, in her book *Fasting Girls, The Emergence of Anorexia Nervosa as a Modern Disease*, quotes Albrecht Von Haller (1708–1777) who wrote, "All medical history from the earliest time is filled with men, but especially women, who for whole entire months, in fact even years, lived without food."

emaciation: Extreme thinness to the point that the body appears to be wasting away from starvation.

Gradually, throughout the seventeenth and eighteenth centuries, abstaining from food was regarded less and less as some sort of miracle and more and more as a medical problem to be observed and treated, if possible. Medical professionals in England, France, and the United States all identified anorexia at about the same time, the 1870s. The best known, Sir William Withey Gull, was a prominent London physician who was also the medical adviser to Queen Victoria's family. In 1873, he labeled the disease anorexia nervosa and gave other physicians a way to tell the difference between the emaciation of anorexia nervosa and emaciation caused by other wasting diseases or biomedical conditions.

Brumberg writes:

Women of means were the first to diet to constrain their appetite, and they began to do so before the sexual and fashion revolutions of the 1920s and the 1960s. In the 1890s Veblen noted that privileged women "[took] thought to alter their persons, so as to conform more nearly to the instructed taste of the time." . . . In bourgeois society it became incumbent upon women to control their appetite in order to encode their body with the correct social messages. Appetite became less of a biological drive and more of a social and emotional instrument.

It became fashionable during this time to look down on "sturdiness" as low class, even vulgar. It was considered far more genteel to eat very little, even to be ill, which was interpreted as being "delicate." As far back as 1863, American writer Hester Pendleton commented, "So perverted are the tastes of some persons that delicacy of constitution is considered a badge of aristocracy, and daughters would feel themselves deprecated by too robust health."
Brumberg elaborates:

bourgeois: The French term for the middle class.

fecundity: The capability to have offspring.

asexuality: Not sexual, sexless.

By eating only tiny amounts of food, young women could disassociate themselves from sexuality and fecundity and they could achieve an unambiguous class identity. The thin body not only implied asexuality and an elevated social address, it was also an expression of intelligence, sensitivity, and morality. Through control of appetite, Victorian girls found a way of expressing a complex of emotional, aesthetic, and class sensibilities.

By the beginning of the twentieth century, affluent young girls felt it was extremely important to be thin. Albutt, in his work *A System of Medicine*, wrote: "Many young women, as their frames develop, fall into a panic fear of obesity, and not only cut down on their food, but swallow vinegar and other alleged antidotes to fatness." In the postindustrial age, our own time, eating disorders have become far removed from the pursuit of spiritual beauty and now seem related to the search for perfection in terms of physical beauty.

Anorexia nervosa came to the attention of the public in a forceful way when Karen Carpenter died of heart failure associated with her battle with the disease in 1983. Carpenter was only thirty-two at the time, a popular singer who often performed with her brother Richard.

At about the same time as Carpenter's tragic death, anorexia nervosa began to show up on television ("The Best Little Girl in the World," 1981; an episode of the program *Fame*), and in novels (*Fly Away Home*, by Marge Piercy; *Second Star to the Right*, by Deborah Hautzig).

Originally, bulimia did not receive as much attention as anorexia, although the disease was known as far back as the nineteenth century. According to Rachel Epstein, in *Eating Habits and Disorders*, Doctors M. Boskind-White and W.C. White Jr. invented and used the term "bulimarexia" in 1976 in their description of people without histories of weight disorders who had bulimic symptoms. In 1979, a doctor named G. F. M. Russell first recognized and named bulimia nervosa as a disorder separate from, though related to, anorexia nervosa. Bulimia nervosa first appeared in the DSM in 1980.

In the early 1980s, personal testimonials from well-known figures who suffered from anorexia or bulimia began to appear. These included novelist Shelia Macleod, Cherry Boone O'Neill, and Jane Fonda. Fonda admitted to bingeing and purging while at Vassar College and during her early film career, and soon autobiographical books from other women with bulimia began to appear.

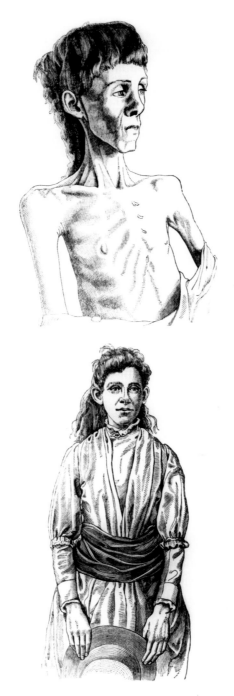

This nineteenth-century medical drawing portrays an anorexic girl before and after treatment.

Looking for a Cause

Even the experts who frequently treat individuals with eating disorders have not yet been able to agree on a cause of eating disorders. Most proposed causes fall into one, or a combination, of three categories.

Biomedical

The people who support a biomedical cause for eating disorders are often researchers or doctors who work in research. They search primarily for problems in the biological processes of their patients, looking for an organic origin. Suggested biomedical causes include hormone imbalance; dysfunction in the satiety center of the hypothalamus (an area that regulates many body functions, including food and water intake, body temperature, respiration, circulation, digestion, and metabolism); damage to the limbic system of the brain, which is thought to control emotions, behavior, and smell; and irregular output of the hormones vasopressin and gonadotropin. More than a decade ago, the National Institutes of Health conducted research that showed an oversecretion of hormones in the brains of patients who were depressed and who had anorexia nervosa.

satiety: The state of having had enough, of being satisfied, full.

pathological: Due to or involving disease.

If anorexia nervosa were shown to have an organic cause, then it would follow that patients have no control over their anorectic behavior, and medical treatment, rather than psychotherapeutic treatment, would be the answer.

Psychological

Some groups propose psychological causes for anorexia nervosa. It has been suggested that anorexia nervosa is a patient's pathological response to entering adolescence, which entails sexual development and becoming independent, among other changes. Sigmund Freud (1856–1939), the Austrian physician and neurologist who founded psychoanalysis, looked at anorectics as girls who feared both sexuality and becoming adult women. Hilde Bruch, in her book *Eating Disorders, Obesity, Anorexia Nervosa, and the Person Within*, follows Freud's line of thinking. She argues, as Brumberg puts it, "the anorectic makes her body a stand-in for the life that she cannot control." Those who adhere to this school of thought point out that girls with anorexia nervosa actually slow down their body's sexual maturing process by refusing to eat. When human females are severely undernourished, their menstrual periods stop, and their bodies remain thin and childlike in appearance.

Anorexia nervosa has at times been categorized with other psychiatric disorders, including schizophrenia, depression, and obsessive-compulsive disorder, in an attempt to understand the origins of the disease. People with eating disorders often have high rates of depression and anxiety, and these will need to be addressed before recovery can take place. Stress and feelings of hopelessness often make the eating disorder's symptoms worse. Mental health professionals have extensively studied the families of individuals with anorexia in an attempt to understand what part, if any, families play in the development of the disorder. Particular attention has been paid to the mothers of girls with anorexia, in an attempt to see if the root cause of this eating disorder could be found in the mother-daughter relationship. Parents who are perfectionistic

psychoanalysis: A psychological treatment method in which detailed accounts of a patient's past are obtained and used to treat contemporary problems.

schizophrenia: A psychological disorder characterized by disturbances in major areas of functioning including, work, school, interpersonal relationships, and self-care. Hallucinations and delusions may also be present.

Our culture's obsession with the "perfect body" may contribute to the prevalence of eating disorders in our society.

and controlling seem to be more likely to have a child with an eating disorder. Gymnasts and ballerinas are also particularly at risk for developing some type of eating disorder.

Cultural

In the mind of many onlookers, it is regarded as a truism that modern North American culture is to blame for anorexia nervosa—at least in part. Given the culture's current obsession with slender bodies, which drives both men and women to spend millions of dollars annually on diet aids, programs, and products, it seems obvious to many that this cultural imbalance must be the primary force behind eating disorders. The media, with its constant succession of slender, attractive people, apparently plays a large part in producing this obsession with beautiful bodies. People with larger bodies are seldom shown on television and only rarely in a positive light. This teaches those who watch that the only females worth imitating are the ones who have slender, beautiful bodies.

truism: A truth that is obvious or well known, a "given."

However, even the cultural model cannot totally explain eating disorders or answer all the questions about them. Eating disorders existed prior to our modern culture, so culture cannot be the sole cause.

While researchers still do not understand what causes eating disorders, they are making progress in treating them. Drug therapy and other treatments cannot cure an eating disorder, but they can help.

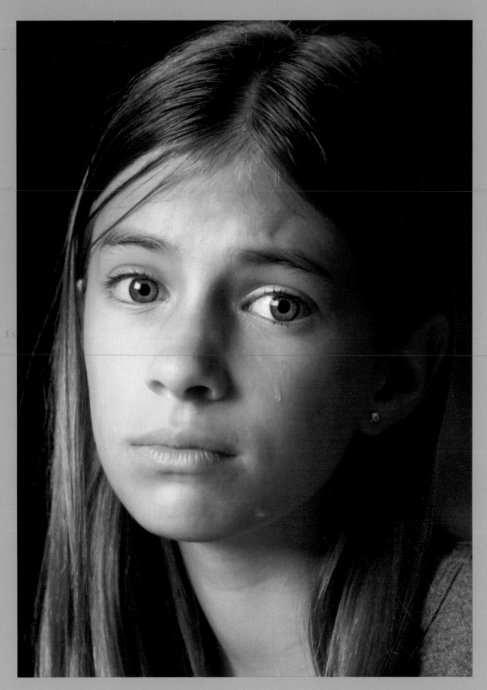

When someone has an eating disorder, she may feel desperate and depressed. Talking to a medical professional is an important first step toward wellness.

Chapter Two

History of the Drug

Date: November 15
Subject: More about me
From: <Happywithme@college.edu>
To: Lindsay<lgirl@compnet.com>

Dear Lindsay,

Thanks for telling me more about yourself. I can see you're having some problems we can discuss. Before I answer your question about how to get people to leave you alone, though, I'll tell you what happened to me so you know where I'm coming from.

I had anorexia nervosa, and later I became bulimic, too. It's a long story—too long for one e-mail—but I'll tell you some about how it started.

All through middle school and high school, I worried that my thighs and hips were too big—you can't carry a lot of weight on a body that's only five-feet-three. But it was never a big deal to me until I went away to college. Once I got there, though, I felt as if everyone was watching me, like they were sizing me up, or judging me for being too big. It didn't help that I was shy, either, or that I suddenly had so many assignments to do and so many papers to write for my classes that I felt as though my life was totally out of control. It was especially hard since I roomed with a girl who stayed a size two no matter what she ate—and she ate a lot, let me tell you. A lot more than me, anyway. Life just isn't fair sometimes!

I ate less and less that first semester to try to lose weight, and by winter break, I had lost twenty-seven pounds. Losing so much weight so fast was a rush for me. I loved feeling as though I was in control of at least some part of my life (even if I couldn't keep up with all those assignments). I also started going out with a really great guy, and he always told me I looked great.

I went on losing weight during second semester, too. I can empathize with what you said about people telling you you're too thin.

No matter how much weight she may lose, a person with an eating disorder is seldom satisfied with the numbers she sees on the bathroom scales.

Despite how thin a person with anorexia may be in reality, all she sees when she looks in the mirror are fat thighs, bulging hips, and a round stomach. When it comes to looking at her own body, her vision of reality is warped.

Everyone started telling me the same thing during that semester. But just like you, when I looked in the mirror, all I could see were my hips and thighs, and they still looked way too fat to me.

Then, about halfway through that semester, I suddenly began to feel like I couldn't control my eating anymore. It was as if my body started crying out for food. I know now that I wasn't feeding myself anywhere near enough to stay healthy, but at the time, I was terrified to eat more. I thought that if I did, I'd gain back every ounce I'd taken off, and lose all the control I had built up.

Let me tell you, Lindsay, college is not a good place to deal with an eating problem. There's food all over the place, all the time. You have to sign up for a certain food plan when you enroll, but it doesn't matter if you miss a meal, because there are dozens of cafés and restaurants around you can go to, and a lot of them are open twenty-four-seven. You can get anything you want any time of the day or night, just about. If I wanted ice cream at eight o'clock in the morning—no problem! Or pancakes and sausage in the middle of the afternoon. There's nobody around to tell you when or how much to eat, either, and all of a sudden, I found myself wanting to eat all the time. I knew what would happen if I did, though, so I absolutely wouldn't give in.

Then I discovered a secret, thanks to my size-two roommate. One day, I cut class and walked in on her when she thought I was at the psych lecture. There were empty food bags and torn wrappers all over her bed—we added it up later and figured out she must have eaten six or seven thousand calories in about an hour—and she was in the bathroom, throwing up. I'd heard of purging, of course. Who hasn't? I'd just never known anyone who did it.

When my roommate saw that I'd caught her in the middle of throwing up, she told me the whole story. At first, purging sounded totally disgusting to me, but when she said she'd been bingeing and purging for over four years, I started to reconsider. I mean, she was really gorgeous. I thought, okay, if she can look this good and eat all she wants, any time she wants, then maybe all those terrible things I've heard about bulimia could be wrong. I tried it myself about a week later—and decided I'd found the answer to my weight problem forever.

Anyway, that's enough about me for now. I'll tell you more about what happened later, but I have to leave for the clinic soon, and I want to answer your question before I go.

I know you're upset that people are bugging you about not eating, Lindsay. It's very annoying when they all keep saying you're too thin, especially when you can look in the mirror and see otherwise. Sometimes, though, a funny thing starts happening when our eating habits get messed up. We don't see ourselves the way the rest of the world sees us. Or maybe even the way we really are.

Here's something to think about. Have you ever gone to one of those fun houses at a carnival? Where they have those mirrors that make you look like you're about four hundred pounds? Or like you're skinnier than a pencil? Neither one of those pictures is the truth, of course, but they look like they're true. Sometimes our minds can get confused about stuff like this, and what we think we see in the mirror isn't the same as what's really there.

Other people can be a help for us when we get to this point, Lindsay, so talking to that doctor again may not be such a bad idea. And you may want to think a little more about what your mother and father are saying. I mean, why would they want to hurt you? I suspect they're just trying to help. For right now, try not to worry about what they want to make you eat or not eat. Just be open to talking with them. Let me know how it goes.

Best wishes to you,
Gina

Date: November 15
Subject: No eating disorder!
From: Lindsay<lgirl@compnet.com>
To: <Happywithme@college.edu>

Gina,

I can tell what you're thinking. I DO NOT have an eating disorder. I've just had some trouble losing weight, that's all. And I DO NOT need to talk to some expert here about it, so you don't ever have to bring that up again, okay?

I just need a friend to talk to—one who understands. Especially now. Since I wrote to you last time, a bad thing happened to my dad's girlfriend. I don't understand what's going on, but I think you may be the right person to ask, since you said you were into the whole bulimia thing.

About a year ago, my dad starting going out with this girl named Maria. She's real tall and thin, with blue eyes and long blond hair. She looks like I always wished I could look (I have black hair and brown eyes, and I'm about five-feet-four, just an inch taller than you). Maria was the first person he went out with that I actually liked, at least a little bit.

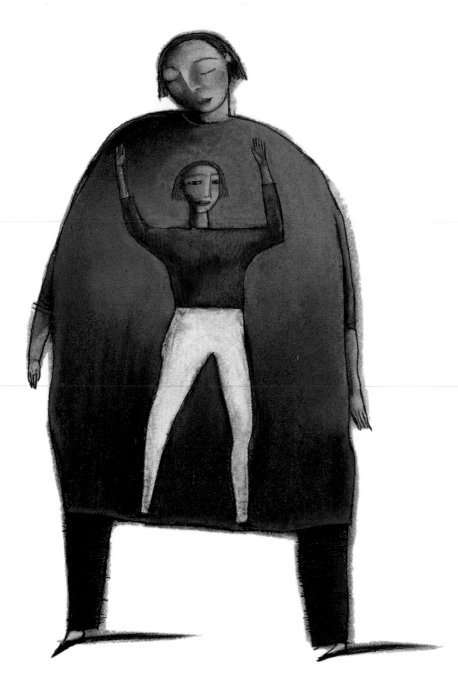

A person with an eating disorder may feel as though she is trapped inside an overweight body. Trying to escape, she may go on harsh diets or exercise regimes.

She was a lot of fun at first. She never got on me about not eating, the way my mom was doing all the time by then. We got to be good friends, and I always had a great time with her. She showed me how to do my makeup different ways and took me to have pedicures—stuff like that.

The funny thing was, she always ate a lot, and she never seemed to have to go on a diet. In fact, she ate everything I'd been staying away from for years, ever since my mom said what she did about being chunky. I'd always tease her and say, "Maria, how on earth can you eat all this stuff and never gain weight?" and she'd be like, "Oh, I guess I just have good genes!"

We laughed about that a lot. It got to be a pretty big joke between us, even though I have to admit I was a little bit jealous, since I was always dieting and exercising and I still never looked like her.

Anyway, this past weekend, my dad and Maria were supposed to take me to an amusement park a couple hours from my house. We were going to spend the whole weekend there and stay in a motel with a hot tub and a big pool.

Then Dad called on Thursday night and canceled everything. First he talked to my mom, then he talked to me and said the trip was off. I was really bummed. "Why can't we go? What happened?" I kept asking him.

At first he wouldn't say much, then he told me that Maria had to go to the emergency room in the middle of the night, and that they were keeping her at the hospital for the next few days. I kept asking him what was wrong with her, but he just kept saying he wasn't completely sure yet and that the doctors had to do a lot of tests, and we should let Maria have her privacy and stuff like that. So I said I'd go down to the hospital and visit her—I mean, she's my friend, too—but he said absolutely not, they wouldn't let me in to see her. Then he said he had to get off the phone but he'd let me know more later.

So I asked my mom if she knew what was going on. She wouldn't answer me at first, but I kept asking and asking, so she finally told me that Maria had bulimia and that something bad happened with her heart because of it. I asked why Dad didn't just tell me that himself, and she said that they had agreed they shouldn't tell me too much about it, since I had an eating problem myself and it might influence me or upset me. That's the way she said it, that I have an "eating problem"!

So now they won't really give me any details about Maria and I'm really scared. I heard some people die from stuff like this. And I really haven't had many other friends since the divorce—I just like to keep to myself pretty much—but Maria's a pretty good friend and I don't want something bad to happen to her.

I'm also pretty angry at her, though. I don't like to think about what she must have been doing all that time to stay so slender. "Good genes," huh?! Why do people have to be such liars anyway?

So I don't really understand much about why she has to be in the hospital. Is there medicine you can take for having an eating problem? Thanks for any information you can give me.

Lindsay

Using drugs that alter the mental state has been a common practice for thousands of years. Alcohol, opiates, cocaine, and peyote are some of the drugs most commonly used for this purpose. These drugs are thought to change behavior by acting on the brain systems that govern behaviors such as sleeping, eating, and sexual behavior. For centuries, people saw the effects of such drugs but had little or no idea of how or why they produced their effects. As researchers and medical health professionals continue to study the brain and its systems, they are gaining more and more insight into how psychiatric drugs work.

For example, reference to a medicine made from the plant Rauwolfia serpentina can be found in ancient texts from India that are more than two thousand years old. According to Bruce M. Cohen, in *Mind and Medicine: Drug Treatments for Psychiatric Illnesses*, this medicine was used to treat symptoms similar to those of schizophrenia and bipolar disorder. Reserpine was probably the active ingredient in this medicine, but it was not until the 1930s that this ingredient was isolated and studied. It was then used to treat psychotic disorders in the 1950s, and did so effectively.

Lithium is a drug often prescribed today for individuals with bipolar disorders. Writings from the time of the Roman Empire recommended that patients with mania use water from specific alkaline springs, water that most likely contained lithium.

Plant preparations containing opium have been used to treat pain for hundreds of years, and in the last two centuries, derivatives of these plants were used to treat psychotic disorders and depression. Coca leaves, which are the source of cocaine, were used around the beginning of the twentieth century as a stimulant and antidepressant. The famous psychotherapist Sigmund Freud was just one of the individuals who chewed coca leaves.

Today, new drugs are discovered and developed in many different ways. Sometimes drugs are discovered when researchers are studying a particular disease, looking for a way to combat or cure it. However, the story behind the development of psychiatric drugs has sometimes been that of medical people stumbling onto a discovery while they were researching something else.

Antipsychotic drugs, for example, were discovered for the most part by anesthesiologists. When these doctors administered certain drugs to surgical patients, they observed the calming effect the drugs had and speculated about other ways the drugs could be used.

The best-known example involves Henri Laborit, a surgeon in Paris. In 1952, Laborit was puzzling over a way to reduce surgical shock in his patients, caused for the most part by anesthesia. He

bipolar disorder: A psychological disorder in which periods of extreme emotional highs alternate with periods of extreme lows.

mania: A mood disorder in which one has feelings of extreme emotional excitement (or "highs"), an inflated sense of self-esteem, and hyperactivity.

anesthesiologists: Doctors who provide the sedation for surgical and other medical procedures.

Drug Discoveries That Changed the World

When Sir Alexander Fleming (1881–1955), a doctor and research bacteriologist at St. Mary's Hospital in London, England, was serving in World War I, he was deeply saddened and distressed by the large number of soldiers who died from bacterial infection of their wounds. As a result, he determined to study bacteria after the war ended. One day in 1928, he noticed mold growing in one of his laboratory cultures and began to observe the culture carefully. He saw that wherever the mold grew, the bacteria were destroyed. He studied and experimented with the mold, and eventually, after many years of research, a powerful antibiotic with great lifesaving potential was developed. The mold was a species of Penicillium, so Sir Fleming named it penicillin, a name now familiar to millions of people around the world.

For other diseases, such as poliomyelitis (polio), antibiotics were not effective. As late as the 1950s, polio was still a dreaded illness that frequently crippled or paralyzed young people. Then Jonas Edward Salk (1914–1995), associate professor of bacteriology and head of the Virus Research Laboratory at the University of Pittsburgh School of Medicine, began research on a polio vaccine and eventually developed one that was effective against all three viruses that cause polio.

felt that if he could use less anesthetic during surgery, his patients could recover more quickly. Since shock was known to result from certain brain chemicals, he decided to try using another chemical to counteract this effect. He tried antihistamines, drugs usually used to fight allergies.

Laborit noticed that, when he gave his patients a strong dose of antihistamines, they no longer seemed anxious about their upcoming surgery. As a result, Laborit could use much less anesthetic during the

Our world has been changed by the scientitsts who researched diligently until they discovered substances with the power to treat diseases.

operation. The effect of the antihistamines was even more far-reaching than what Laborit originally intended, affecting his patients' mental state so strongly that the doctor began to think these drugs—especially chlorpromazine—might be of some use in the field of psychiatry.

The most popular psychiatric treatments at that time, however, were electric shock or various psychotherapies. "No one in his right mind in psychiatry was working with drugs," Canadian psychiatrist Heinz Lehmann says of that period. But when psychiatrist Pierre Deniker learned what had happened with the chlorpromazine, he ordered a supply of the drug to try on his most agitated, uncontrollable patients. The results were amazing. Patients who had needed to be restrained because of their violent behavior, as well as patients who had stood in one spot without moving for weeks, could now be left without supervision and could actually respond to other people. Some people who had been ill for years were able to return to work.

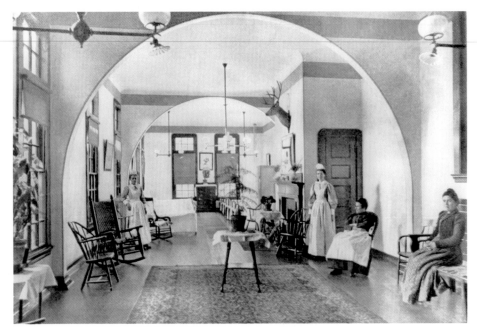

In the nineteenth century, before psychiatric drugs were discovered, insane asylums sought to treat people with psychiatric disorders by removing them from the rest of society.

Between the years of 1904 and 1955, severe mental illness had been growing in America, from two out of a thousand people institutionalized in mental hospitals to four out of a thousand. There was little available to help the mentally ill, and they were routinely "warehoused" in state institutions.

At the same time, an American drug company named SmithKline was hoping to expand its line of drugs. SmithKline heard about chlorpromazine's amazing results, bought the rights to the drug from a European company called Rhone-Poulenc, and marketed it in the United States as an antivomiting medication. SmithKline tried to convince American medical schools and university psychology departments to test the drug for psychiatric use, but chlorpromazine was considered just another sedative. Academics and doctors continued to favor treating mental disorders solely with psychoanalysis and behaviorism.

SmithKline then asked Dr. Deniker to help influence doctors in America to use the drug, and he agreed. The first successes for chlorpromazine hydrochloride came in state institutions, where test results seemed miraculous. When chlorpromazine was approved by the U.S. Food and Drug Administration in 1954, it had a huge effect on thousands, even millions, of people with mental disorders. It decreased the intensity of schizophrenia symptoms such as hallucinations and delusions. It calmed people without sedating them and, in many cases, allowed them to lead an almost normal life. By 1964, fifty million people around the world had taken the drug, and SmithKline had doubled their revenues three times.

behaviorism: A school of psychological thought in which only those behaviors that can be objectively measured are of concern.

hallucinations: The perception of objects or sounds that do not exist in reality.

delusions: A persistent, false belief about oneself or others.

sedating: Having a calming, tranquilizing effect.

Guidelines for Getting Psychiatric Drugs

1. Advanced practice nurses such as clinical nurse specialists, nurse practitioners, or psychiatrists can prescribe medication in most states within the United States.

2. If there are clinical nurse specialists, psychiatric nurse practitioners, or psychiatrists available in your area, they have specialized training in the psychopharmacological and psychotherapeutic diagnosis and treatment of psychiatric disorders. If you do not have access to a professional who specializes in psychiatric disorders, your medical doctor may be able to help you.

3. Discuss the diagnosis and treatment options with your treating physician or advanced practice nurse. You should ask lots of questions about the medication, side effects, risks, benefits, and alternatives to treatment, how long it takes for the medicine to work, whether or not you can stop the medication abruptly, what to do if you miss a dose, if taking over-the-counter medications such as cold remedies are contraindicated, and so on.

4. Your initial evaluation appointment usually takes approximately an hour. You should bring any previous psychiatric testing, or records from previous doctors who have treated you for this condition in the past, and what medications and doses you have taken. It is also helpful to keep a diary of symptoms on a daily basis, including any triggers, mood fluctuations, trouble sleeping, eating, etc. This is helpful for the clinician to gain an understanding of what the real issues are and any patterns that are present.

5. Ask the treating clinician to educate you about the diagnosis, how she arrived at it, what the prognosis for this disorder is, and what types of help are available: groups, books to read, etc.

6. Second opinions are always an option if you have concerns about the diagnosis and treatment plan. You may want to seek an expert in this particular disorder to confirm the diagnosis and treatment plan if you are not improving.
7. It is important to assess the risk/benefit ratio of treatment: How impairing is the disorder? What are the side effects of the medication? What are the other treatment options?
8. In many cases, it is helpful to have family involved in treatment. Discuss this with your clinician to see if it might be helpful in your particular case.
9. It is important to keep follow-up appointments, as adjustments in medication may be needed. The clinician will assess improvement and side effects and be constantly monitoring your progress in direct relationship to the side effects (risk/benefit ratio). The frequency of follow-up visits will vary depending on the severity of your disorder and your response to treatment.

Although side effects and other drawbacks associated with chlorpromazine eventually came to light, the dramatic effects of this chemical on the brain led people to begin thinking differently about brain function and behavior.

For instance, since one side effect of chlorpromazine was to produce effects similar to those of Parkinson's disease, researchers began to consider the possibility that similar chemicals might be involved in natural Parkinson's disease and that it might be possible to counteract them. This type of thinking eventually resulted in understanding the role of dopamine and other neurotransmitters (see chapter 3 for an explanation of how neurotransmitters work in the central nervous system), an advance that has had great impact on the treatment of mental disorders. When the

Drug Approval

Before a drug can be marketed in the United States, it must be officially approved by the Food and Drug Administration (FDA). Today's FDA is the primary consumer protection agency in the United States. Operating under the authority given it by the government, and guided by laws established throughout the twentieth century, the FDA has established a rigorous drug approval process that verifies the safety, effectiveness, and accuracy of labeling for any drug marketed in the United States.

While the United States has the FDA for the approval and regulation of drugs and medical devices, Canada has a similar organization called the Therapeutic Product Directorate (TPD). The TPD is a division of Health Canada, the Canadian government department of health. The TPD regulates drugs, medical devises, disinfectants, and sanitizers with disinfectant claims. Some of the things that the TPD monitors are quality, effectiveness, and safety. Just as the FDA must approve new drugs in the United States, the TPD must approve new drugs in Canada before those drugs can enter the market.

antipsychotic drugs were observed to relieve psychotic symptoms such as hallucinations and delusions in patients with schizophrenia, researchers found that their effect was due to the drug's ability to block dopamine receptors in the brain. As a result, scientists began to wonder if schizophrenia, or any part of it, could be a result of an excess of dopamine. Operating on the same principle, scientists then questioned whether depression could be related to a lack of the neurotransmitters serotonin and noradrenaline, and if anxiety could be caused by a lack of GABA (a neurotransmitter called gamma-aminobutyric acid).

With this new and ever-growing understanding of how medications can affect the brain, drug companies went on to develop and market other medicines to treat psychiatric problems. More antipsychotics were developed after chlorpromazine, including other standard antipsychotics and later the atypical antipsychotics.

The benzodiazepine anxiolytics (such as Valium and Xanax) were first developed in the late 1950s. Chlordiazepoxide (Librium) and diazepam (Valium) were among the most popular benzodiazepines and were very effective in treating anxiety. However, all the drugs in this class have the potential to be addictive, so they must be used carefully, under the close supervision of a medical professional.

Some of the antidepressant drugs called monoamine oxidase inhibitors (MAOIs) were discovered as a result of tuberculosis treatment. When tuberculosis patients were given an antibiotic called iproniazide, those who were also depressed experienced relief from their depression. The same medication helped alleviate problems the patients had with appetite, energy, and sleep. When studies were done, iproniazide was shown to produce these effects by inhibiting the enzyme called monoamine oxidase. This sets in motion a process leading to a higher concentration of neurotransmitters called the monoamines (norepinephrine, serotonin, and dopamine) in the brain, thus helping relieve depression. (See chapter three for more details on how different classes of drugs work.) Because iproniazide was so successful in treating depression, more drugs of the MAOI type were developed. Today, the MAOIs phenelzine sulfate (Nardil) and isocarboxazid are two of the psychiatric medications most frequently used to treat bulimia.

In the last half of the twentieth century, while researchers were searching for drugs to use in treating psychotic disorders, they observed that one of the compounds they tested seemed to help depressed patients substantially. This compound, imipramine (Tofranil), the first of the tricyclic antidepressants (TCAs), has been a highly successful antidepressant and is still used today to treat

Researchers developed the first benzodiazepines in the late 1950s.

patients who have failed to respond to other drugs. It is also used to treat Tourette's syndrome and bulimia, although these are "off-label" treatments. Given the success of imipramine, researchers went on to develop many more drugs in this class.

During the 1980s, pharmaceutical companies began working on a new class of antidepressants that would have fewer side effects than the TCAs. They designed a new class of drugs that blocked the reuptake of serotonin, but not norepinephrine, and called them selective serotonin reuptake inhibitors (SSRIs). The first of these drugs was called fluoxetine (Prozac), and several other SSRIs were then developed, including

Tourette's syndrome: A neurological disorder characterized by repetitive, involuntary motor and verbal tics.

reuptake: The process by which neurons pick up neurotransmitters.

Brand Name vs. Generic Name

Talking about psychiatric drugs can be confusing, because every drug has at least two names: its "generic name" and the "brand name" that the pharmaceutical company uses to market the drug. Generic names come from the drugs' chemical structures, while brand names are used by drug companies in order to inspire public recognition and loyalty for their products.

Here are the brand names and generic names for some common psychiatric drugs:

Elavil®	amitriptyline hydrochloride
Librium®	chlorodiazepoxide
Marplan®	isocarboxazid
Nardil®	phenelzine sulfate
Norpramin®	desipramine hydrochloride
Paxil®	paroxetine hydrochloride
Periactin®	cyproheptadine hydrochloride
Prozac®	fluoxetine hyrdrochloride
Tofranil®	imipramine hydrochloride
Valium®	diazepam
Xanax®	alprazolam
Zofran®	ondansetron hydrochloride
Zoloft®	sertraline hydrochloride

sertraline (Zoloft), and paroxetine (Paxil), that have also been successful. Prozac has had such good success in treating bulimia that it is now approved by the FDA (the Food and Drug Administration) as a treatment for bulimia. Although no drug has been very effective in treating anorexia, Prozac has proven to have limited success in this area. SSRIs are generally used at higher doses when treating an eating disorder.

Looking Inside the Brain

Advances made in recent years in imaging living, intact brains have helped scientists better understand how this organ works. With more understanding in this area, new drugs that affect the brain can be developed. While it is relatively simple to tell what is going on in other body organs by means of a blood test, information about the brain is not so easily accessible. Because of what scientists refer to as the blood-brain barrier, many medicines are not able to get into the brain. Now, however, the following valuable methods for "seeing" the brain have been developed:

- CAT (computerized axial tomography) reveals brain structures without harming the patient.
- MRI (magnetic resonance imaging) gives highly refined pictures of the brain using magnetic fields and without using radiation.
- PET (positron emission tomography) and SPECT (single-photon emission computed tomography) reveal brain structure and also show metabolic activity in various parts of the brain (brain chemicals and their receptors).

With the development of these latest imaging techniques, scientists can now inject chemicals labeled with tiny amounts of radioactivity into a person's bloodstream. They can then watch where the chemicals go inside the brain and to what receptors they bind.

Research continues on other fronts as well. With the advent of genetic research, molecular geneticists have linked some psychiatric diseases, such as schizophrenia and bipolar disorder, to abnormal genes. Other researchers have developed methods to study psychotherapies under controlled conditions. This means that psychotherapies and drug therapies can now be compared scientifically so that practitioners will soon have a better understanding of the uses and the limitations of both types of treatment.

Although many of the modern psychiatric drugs were discovered by accident, researchers and pharmaceutical companies have used the knowledge gained from those early discoveries to develop many helpful medications. Research in this field is ongoing, and new drugs are being developed and tested all the time. When used in conjunction with other treatment (such as counseling with a nutritionist or family and individual therapy), psychiatric medications can make a tremendous difference in the lives of many people diagnosed with eating disorders and other mental disorders. It's a long process, though—there is no quick cure.

blood-brain barrier: Barrier created by the walls of the brain capillaries that prevents most proteins and drugs from passing from the blood into the brain tissue and cerebrospinal fluid.

radioactivity: The capability of certain elements to spontaneously emit energy particle by disintegrating the nucleus.

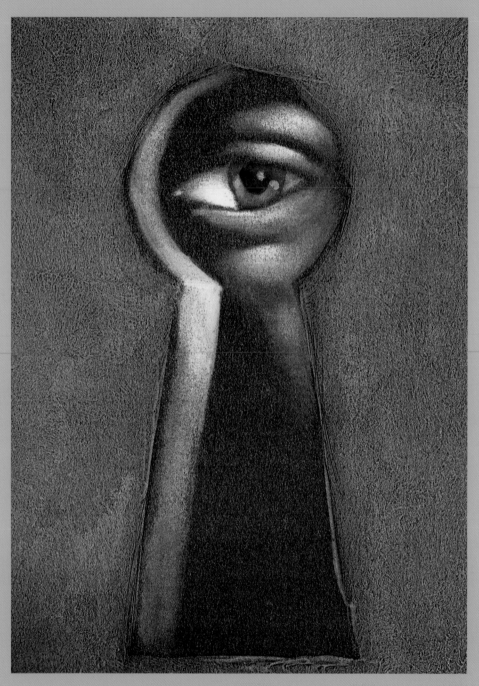

Psychiatric drugs may help individuals with eating disorders gain insight into their condition. Although these drugs provide no magic answers, they may offer a key that leads to healing.

Chapter Three

How Does the Drug Work?

Date: November17
Subject: Re: No eating disorder!
From: <Happywithme@college.edu>
To: Lindsay<lgirl@compnet.com>

Dear Lindsay,

I'm really sorry to hear about Maria's problem.

You mentioned that people can die from eating disorders, and you're right, unfortunately. But the good news is that Maria's doing exactly what she needs to be doing right now—getting help. I'll keep hoping with you that she will recover completely, as many people do.

You asked why Maria has to be in a hospital. I can't tell you for sure exactly what's going on with her, of course. But if she's developed an electrolyte imbalance or dehydration—that can happen from making yourself throw up frequently or from misusing laxatives—it could affect her heart rhythm, a problem that can cause sudden death. Sometimes they have to put people in the hospital for this, to stabilize their heart rhythm and get their electrolytes back into balance, and to get them rehydrated. Maybe that's what they're doing for Maria. Human bodies were never meant to throw up most of the food we eat, so bulimia can cause a lot of different problems. Later on, I'll tell you a few of the things that happened to me after I was bulimic for about two years.

rehydrated: To restore water or other fluids to something.

But of course, I never thought of the bad consequences when I started purging. Like I told you before, I just thought I'd found the magic answer to the weight loss problem. I'd been starving myself for so long that it seemed like heaven to get to eat all I wanted and

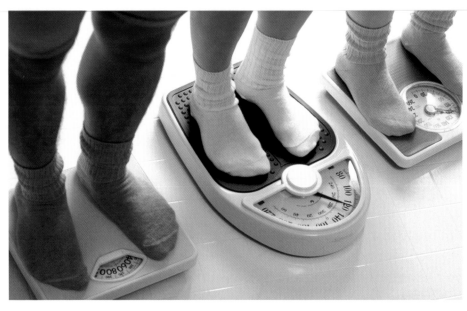

Many of us are unhappy with our weight; but that doesn't mean we all have eating disorders. An eating disorder is a serious psychiatric condition that requires professional treatment.

then be able to just get rid of it—no calories in my stomach, no fat on my hips! But it didn't really solve any of my problems. It just took my mind off them for a short time.

Looking back, I'm not sure which came first—the bulimia or the anxiety problems. I was getting more and more anxious about my classes at school. The workload was so heavy that I could never catch up. I'd been focused on getting good grades all through high school, and now I started having scary thoughts all the time, like, "If I can't pass these freshman courses, how will I ever do upper-level work? If I can't pass college, how will I ever get a decent job? How will I support myself?" The thoughts started taking up more and more of my time, and I had a lot of trouble sleeping. Bingeing and purging took my mind off all this for a little while, but it got harder and harder to hide.

My roommate the year before was the only person who knew I was into purging, and of course, she was into it, too. But when I got a new roommate the next fall, I had to get really clever about keeping my secret. Purging is not exactly the kind of thing you want to tell everybody you're doing, so I ended up sneaking around a lot. I had to always be thinking ahead about things, like, "When would my roommate be at classes or the library? Would she be there long enough that I'd have time to eat everything I wanted to eat back in our room and still get rid of it all?" Plus, it's not very pleasant in a bathroom where somebody's been throwing up, so I had to make sure there'd be time to clean up everything before she got back. I had to plan every binge down to the last detail.

There was always this element of fear that I'd be caught. I grew more and more anxious about it—I was especially nervous that the guy I was dating would find out. Not many guys get involved in bulimia or anorexia—only about ten percent of people with eating disorders are male—and I didn't think he'd understand at all.

So, even though bulimia can seem like it helps at first, in the end it makes life awfully hard. I'm sorry that Maria's struggling with it. When she gets out of the hospital, I'd be glad to e-mail her, too, if you want me to.

In his book *The New Psychiatry*, Dr. Jack M. Gorman stresses the importance of a patient's knowing whether or not the prescribed medication is working. "The one advantage of medication over other forms of psychiatric treatment is that an effect is usually discernible in a matter of weeks; no one should ever continue to take medication unless it is clear there is a benefit," he says. In order to assess this, he encourages patients to realize that psychiatric drugs cannot: improve one's basic personality; give one job success or a better marriage; make one smarter, more athletic, or a better parent. Instead, their effect—usually quite concrete—is to relieve and often eliminate specific symptoms. For those with bulimia, these specific symptoms include bingeing. The drugs used to treat bulimia are working when they help the patient to lessen the number of times they binge and purge. As anxiety, depression, and obsessions are controlled by medication, the patient has more strength to deal with her disorder.

For right now, though, Lindsay, let me say something about your question about why people have to be such liars. I don't know Maria, so I can't answer for her, of course. But when I was bulimic, I lied so much to cover up what I was doing that I even started lying to myself. After a while, I don't think I realized I was lying anymore. I just kept telling myself, "Okay, this'll be the last time I ever do this. One more binge and I quit." I'd talk to myself in the mirror, you know? Like, "Gina, I promise that tomorrow, after this last binge, I'll go to the eating disorders clinic and tell them I need help." Then I'd feel okay about going to the store and buying all that food and planning my binge—because I knew this would be the last time.

Except it never was.

So don't get too angry at Maria about lying to you, if you can help it. She may not even realize she's lying anymore. And if she's

Psychiatric drugs can help manage some of the symptoms of an eating disorder. They cannot, however, make a person magically feel good about her body. Being comfortable with who we are—physically, emotionally, intellectually—is important to good health.

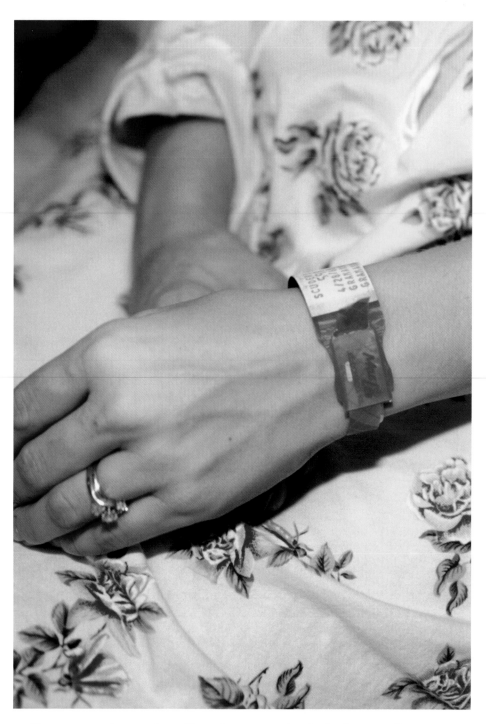

Treatment for eating disorders may include hospitalization.

Public Opinion

Readers can observe how public opinion toward overweight people progressed throughout the first half of the twentieth century by the following three quotes:

> "To judge by the efforts of the majority of women to attain slender and sylph-like proportions, one would fancy it is a crime to be fat."
> (*Vogue*, 1902)
> "There is one crime against the modern ethics of beauty which is unpardonable; far better it is to commit any number of petty crimes than to be guilty of the sin of growing fat."
> (*Vogue*, 1918)
> "An abundance of fat is something repulsive and not in accord with the principles that rule our conception of the beautiful."
> (Helena Rubenstein, *The Art of Feminine Beauty*, 1930)

Adapted from *Fasting Girl: The Emergence of Anorexia Nervosa as a Modern Disease*, by Joan Jacobs Brumberg.

like I was, she was probably way too ashamed to tell you about the purging.

Before I sign off, Lindsay, there's something else I need to say. I'm just going to be completely straight with you about this, even though I suspect you won't want to hear it. Bulimia is bad enough, but anorexia kills 10 to 20 percent of the people who get hospitalized with it. They die from starvation or complications like an electrolyte imbalance or because they commit suicide. You're probably wondering why I'm bringing this up, since Maria has bulimia, not anorexia. It's because, from everything you're telling me, I'm even more concerned about you than I am about Maria. It's not unusual for people to have anorexia and not even realize it at first. They usually say the same kind of things you're saying: "I just have a problem losing weight; I just want to lose a few more pounds; I look fat when I look in the mirror; everybody's always telling me I'm too thin."

I feel as if we've gotten to be friends, Lindsay, even though I haven't met you personally. And I care about what happens to you. Nobody was there for me when I was going through bulimia, and I think it took me longer to get help because of that.

But I want to be here for you. Would you please think more about talking to the doctor again? Or to someone else who works with eating disorders? There are medicines and other treatments that can help you.

Caring about you,
Gina

How Do Psychiatric Drugs Work?

According to Bruce M. Cohen in *Mind and Medicine: Drug Treatments for Psychiatric Illnesses*, "Drugs and medications can change the patterns of firing in neural circuits and the tone of neural activity in the brain. By doing so, they can alter those aspects of consciousness that make us most human."

In order to understand how psychiatric medications help in the treatment of eating disorders and other mental disorders, it is important to first have a basic understanding of how the human brain operates. The sheer complexity of the human brain is astounding. Inside are millions and millions of neurons—specialized brain cells that are capable of passing messages to other neurons. There are so many neurons in our brains that if all the neurons with their axons from a single human brain were stretched out end to end it would go to the moon and back.

Researchers work to understand how the brain works, so that they can determine the chemicals that can treat psychiatric disorders.

Not all FDA-approved drugs are approved for people of all ages. The FDA can only approve a drug for use in the age group in which it was studied. Because the use of psychotropic medications is relatively new, many of these chemicals have not been studied in children and adolescents. Congress recently passed legislation requiring that American drug manufacturers conduct research studies in children and adolescents before it can gain FDA approval for use in adults. Lack of FDA approval, however, does not mean that the drug is unsafe or cannot be used in children. In many cases, a wealth of data supports safety and efficacy in children. "Off-label use" of these psychotropic medications is currently the standard of care in many cases.

The brain does not operate alone. It is part of the central nervous system (CNS), which also includes the spinal cord. Between the brain and the central nervous system, each individual has billions of neurons, both sensory and motor. Our five senses—sight, hearing, smell, touch, and taste—feed information from the outside world to the brain by way of the sensory neurons. Motor neurons respond to this information by making the muscles of our bodies move.

When our bodies are in danger, this system of motor and sensory neurons works to move us out of harm's way. If we burn a finger on a hot iron, the nerve cells in that finger instantly conduct a message about the situation along their axons to the spinal cord. Information is then relayed to other neurons, which send information back to the finger, telling it to move very quickly in order to avoid further burning. All of this happens in a flash. At the same time, important information about hot irons is somehow stored in the memory, so that we are careful in the future to protect our fingers near hot irons.

How do messages, or neural impulses, travel through the body to the spine or brain? Much of the answer lies in the structure of the neuron itself. In one area of each neuron the cell body sends out dendrites, projections that look like tiny twigs. In another area of the neuron the cell body extends a long, thin filament called an axon. At the end of the axon are several terminal buttons. The terminal buttons lie on the dendrites of another neuron so that each neuron functions as a link in the communication chain. The chain does not run in just one direction, however. Because each neuron is in contact with many other neurons, the CNS is like a vast mesh or web of interconnected groups of neurons. The communication connections and interconnections possible between these millions of neurons—with their cell bodies, axons, and dendrites—is an amazing thing to consider.

Brain cells communicate by sending electrical signals from neuron to neuron. Axons and dendrites are very close together but do not actually touch other neurons. In between these cells is a minute space called a synapse. Nerve impulses travel through this space, jumping the space in much the same way an electrical current would. When a message is to be transferred, a neuron "fires," and its terminal buttons release chemicals called neurotransmitters (biochemical substances such as norepinephrine and dopamine), that make jumping the synapse possible. When an electrical signal comes to the end of one neuron, the cell fires, secreting the proper neurotransmitter into the synapse. This chemical messenger then crosses from the presynaptic neuron (the brain cell sending the message) to the postsynaptic neuron (the brain cell receiving the message), where it binds itself to the appropriate chemical receptor and influences the behavior of this second neuron. Neurotransmitters can influence the behavior of the postsynaptic neuron by either transmitting the message or by inhibiting the passage of the message.

When the neurotransmitter binds to the receptors, other processes are set in motion in the postsynaptic brain cell, either exciting it to keep sending the message along or inhibiting it to stop the transmission of the message. After the impulse is passed from one neuron to another, the neurotransmitter falls off the receptor and back into the synapse. There it is either taken back into the presynaptic neuron (a kind of neuron recycling), broken down by enzymes and discarded to spinal fluid surrounding the brain, or it re-attaches itself to the receptor, thus strengthening the original signal traveling from the presynaptic neuron.

The brain contains at least one hundred billion synapses. Researchers speculate that there may be hundreds of different neurotransmitters. And many neurons respond to more than one neurotransmitter. Psychiatric drugs operate in this complex brain environment, usually by influencing neurotransmitters.

According to Bruce Cohen in *Social Research*, "drugs appear to act on systems built into the brain to modulate behaviors associated with eating, sleeping, sexual activity, or other drives and rewards. Co-opting receptors and processes developed to respond to internal chemical messages, these external agents alter arousal, attention, emotional state, and thinking."

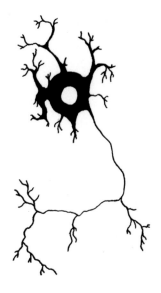

A neuron.

There are different classes of drugs, and each class of drugs appears to operate in different ways. Professional medical workers are quick to say that no drug cures eating disorders. However, some drugs have proven to be valuable in the process of treating these disorders, usually in conjunction with other types of treatment. In *Current Treatments of Obsessive-Compulsive Disorder,* Pato and Zohar write that the evidence shows "anorexia nervosa and bulimia nervosa respond differently to pharmacotherapy, with bulimia responding to all types of antidepressants, albeit with an often modest response, whereas anorexia responds preferentially to serotonin reuptake inhibitors." The drugs currently being used to treat eating disorders are discussed below.

Drugs for Anorexia Nervosa

Although psychiatric drugs are of limited value in the treatment of anorexia nervosa, fluoxetine (Prozac), one of the SSRIs, has been used in some cases. However, in some instances, Prozac can cause weight loss, which would be an undesireable side effect for patients with anorexia. Edward Drummond, M.D., in *The Complete Guide to Psychiatric Drugs*, names cyproheptadine (Periactin), an antihistamine, as one medication that can aid some anorexic patients in gaining weight. Antihistamines reduce excessive mucus secretions and so are most frequently used in treating respiratory infections and allergies. However, because they also make people tired, they have a sedative quality and are sometimes used to reduce feelings of anxiety. (Many people with an eating disorder find that their anxiety levels tend to elevate before and after meals.) Cyproheptadine acts by blocking postsynaptic histamine and serotonin receptors.

Drummond also suggests that antidepressants may help some individuals eat more and that the atypical antipsychotics may provide a little help in se-

pharmacotherapy: The use of drugs to treat illness.

sedative: Something that soothes and quiets.

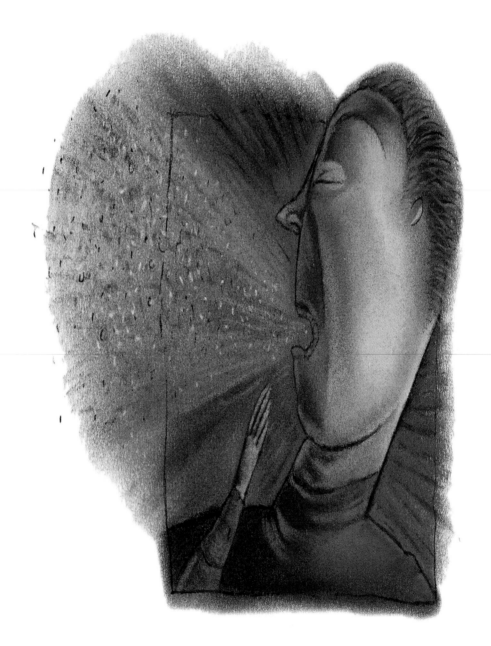

Antihistimanes are medications developed for the treatment of respiratory infections and allergies. These drugs are also sometimes used to reduce anxious feelings.

vere cases of anorexia. Atypical antipsychotics work by blocking a subset of dopamine and serotonin receptors. These are particularly helpful in patients with mood swings and racing thoughts.

Drugs for Bulimia Nervosa

Tricyclic Antidepressants

TCAs include desipramine (Norpramin), imipramine (Tofranil), and amitriptyline (Elavil). The TCAs seem to produce their effects by operating on the monoamine neurotransmitters. They block the reuptake of norepinephrine and serotonin into presynaptic neurons. They appear to act in a similar, but weaker, way on serotonin and to have little effect on dopamine. This means that the TCAs actually increase the amount of serotonin and norepinephrine available to brain receptors. These neurotransmitters are vital for many functions and have been related to depression, anger, and impulsivity. Desipramine, imipramine, and amitriptyline are not approved for patients under the age of twelve, but "off-label" use is common. If a patient is suicidal, TCAs would not be an appropriate medication, since overdoses are often lethal.

Selective Serotonin Reuptake Inhibitors

One of the most common of these drugs is fluoxetine (Prozac). While Prozac is the the only approved medication for children as young as eight, but it is also approved by the FDA for the treatment of bulimia in adults. Like the TCAs, drugs in the SSRI class increase the amount of certain neurotransmitters available to brain receptors. SSRIs usually work with fewer and less serious side effects than do some of the TCAs. As the name of this class of drugs suggests, SSRIs work by specifically inhibiting the reuptake of serotonin, thus making more of this vital neurotransmitter available in the brain. They do not block the reuptake of norepinephrine.

Serotonin Reuptake

To visualize the process of serotonin reuptake, imagine a vacuum cleaner that sucks the serotonin back into the cell. SSRIs block the vacuum, the way your family's vacuum cleaner might get blocked if you were to suck up a sock or some other large object. When the vacuum is clogged, nothing else can get sucked up. When this happens in the cell, it leaves the serotonin in the synapsis to be used again.

Monoamine Oxidase Inhibitors [MAOIs]

These drugs include phenelzine (Nardil) and isocarboxazid (Marplan). MAOIs inhibit monoamine oxidase, which is an enzyme that breaks down dopamine, epinephrine, norepinephrine, and serotonin. As a result, the brain has higher levels of these neurotransmitters, which are used as chemical messengers in the brain. Neither phenelzine nor isocarboxazid is FDA approved for use in patients under the age of sixteen. They are not prescribed often for eating disorders because of the risks and dietary restrictions entailed with their use.

Other Drugs Used to Treat Bulimia

Modest results in treating patients with bulimia by using ondansetron (Zofran), a selective serotonin receptor antagonist, have recently been reported. Ondansetron was originally developed to treat the vomiting that is associated with chemotherapy and radiation.

receptor: Something that acts as a receiver.

All of the medications named above have at least some effect on the problem of eating disorders, though with several of them, the effect is quite small. While psychiatric drugs cannot stand alone as a sole effective treatment for eating disorders, they can in many instances contribute to a patient's ability to regain health. Their effectiveness, when used in conjunction with other treatments, has been demonstrated by numerous studies.

Many people with eating disorders fail to recognize the seriousness of their disorder. They do not really see what their mirror tells them!

Chapter Four

Treatment Description

Date: November 20
Subject: Please listen to me
From: Lindsay<lgirl@compnet.com>
To: <Happywithme@college.edu>

Gina,

Didn't you listen to what I said? In case you didn't, I'll copy and paste my exact words on the subject:

"I DO NOT have an eating disorder, I just have trouble losing weight. And I DO NOT need to talk to some expert here about it, so you don't ever have to bring that up again, okay?"

I have enough on my mind with Maria's situation, not to mention all the pressure I'm getting from my parents. I don't mean to be rude, Gina, but I don't need pressure from you, too.

Lindsay

Date: November 21
Subject: Re: Please listen to me
From: <Happywithme@college.edu>
To: Lindsay<lgirl@compnet.com>

Dear Lindsay,

I don't want to put pressure on you.
On the other hand, though, I wouldn't be much of a friend if I didn't tell you the truth, would I?
How's Maria doing?

A person with an eating disorder may resist help because she cannot believe the truth that others tell her.

With best wishes for you,
Gina

Date: December 16
Subject: Wondering how you are
From: <Happywithme@college.edu>
To: Lindsay<lgirl@compnet.com>

Dear Lindsay,

It's been several weeks since I've heard from you, so I'm just checking to see how you're doing. And how Maria is, of course.

Best wishes,
Gina

Date: December 17
Subject: Re: Wondering how you are
From: Lindsay<lgirl@compnet.com>
To: <Happywithme@college.edu>

Dear Gina,

Sorry I was so upset with you in my last letter. I appreciate the fact that you tried to help. (But I still haven't changed my mind about talking to the doctor.) I haven't written to you because I've been kind of down. I'm not even very interested in exercising anymore. And school, of course, is a total bore.

Things at home are not exactly wonderful, either. I read on one of the pro-ana websites that smoking is a good way to keep your weight down, so I tried it. My mother found out and acted like I killed somebody. Talk about being grounded for life!

Maria got out of the hospital, but my dad decided he doesn't want to see her anymore, which I think is awful. I mean, he always wanted her to be thin, right? He would never have dated her if she

High Risk for Eating Disorders

Young people involved in athletics and dancing may face particular dangers in regard to eating habits because of the emphasis placed on being thin to achieve success. Competition itself can cause stress, and that stress is often added to a mix that already includes all the relationship issues, peer pressure, and family problems that so often accompany growing up.

In some cases, athletes and dancers who remain very thin are praised by coaches and parents. For some young people, this provides an excuse to continue engaging in destructive eating behaviors and compulsive exercise. Even among those who do not have an eating disorder, eating habits may be disturbed by the constant quest for extreme thinness.

Disordered eating patterns can interfere with nutrition and well-being. According to the Something Fishy website, "dancers, runners, gymnasts and wrestlers seem to be at an elevated risk of serious injury or death because of their desire to lose weight extremely rapidly directly prior to an event." (www.something-fishy.org)

wasn't, I know that for sure. Now that he knows what she was doing to get thin, he doesn't want anything more to do with her. I'm not even speaking to him.

When Maria got out of the hospital, she went away to one of those clinics where they help people with bulimia, probably like the one where you work. I haven't seen her at all, but she sends me an e-mail about once a week. She said they've put her on an eating plan to make sure she gets all the nutrients she needs, and they make sure she doesn't do anything to get rid of it. And she has to meet with a therapist and talk a long time every day. They're also giving her some medicine called Prozac to help her stop the binge-ing and purging. (I could hardly believe it, but my mom told me last week that Maria was doing the binge-and-throw-up thing three or four times a day. That made me really, really sad when I heard it. I mean, how did she even have time to have a life?)

Anyway, I didn't know they could give you Prozac to help with bulimia. Have you ever heard of that?

I hope you're doing okay,
Lindsay

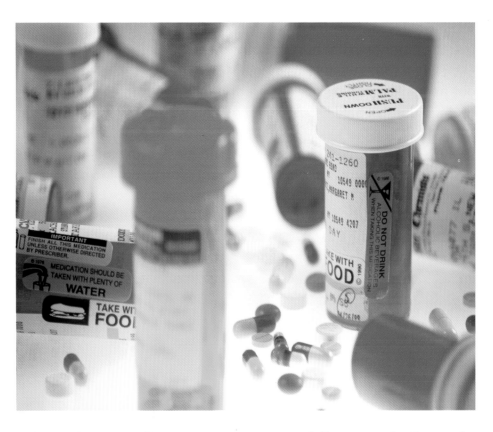

When taking any drug, it is important to follow exactly the medi-cation's instructions.

Date: December 18
Subject: Welcome back
From: <Happywithme@college.edu>
To: Lindsay<lgirl@compnet.com>

Dear Lindsay,

I was so glad to hear from you, girl! I'm sorry about everything that's happening with Maria, but I know the treatment program will help her. Those meetings you mentioned that she's having with the therapist are very important. She'll get to talk through a lot of the feelings inside her that might be contributing to her bulimia. The therapist will help her find different ways to deal with those feelings. See, some people do the binge-and-purge thing so they don't have to feel the emotions that hurt or scare them.

I know that's what I was doing. When the guy I was dating found out about my purging, he did pretty much the same thing your father did. He just said I must be "sick" and walked away. After that, I started purging every day, sometimes twice. I just couldn't let myself face everything that was happening: this guy leaving me, my grades at college sliding way down, the constant worry about food. When I was planning and carrying out a binge, my mind was all wrapped up in that, and I didn't have to think about the other things. You asked how Maria had time to have a life with all that binge-and-purge stuff going on, and you were smart to see that. I know that my own bulimia started taking up so much of my time that I hardly ever saw friends, and I often had to cut classes.

And then weird things started happening to my body: I got two really bad toothaches, so I went to the dentist and found out I—who never had a single cavity while I was growing up—now had several. I thought he'd just fix them and that would be the end of it, but he showed me how some of my teeth were chipping and how the enamel was wearing off in some places. That was from all the throwing up. Sorry to be gross, Lindsay, but the stomach acid in all that vomit is really hard on your teeth.

When someone is being treated for an eating disorder, each meal may be filled with conflicting internal messages. For instance, a person with bulimia may want to binge on sweets instead of maintaining a healthy diet, while someone with anorexia may be tempted to refuse food altogether. Both must learn not to listen to the mental messages.

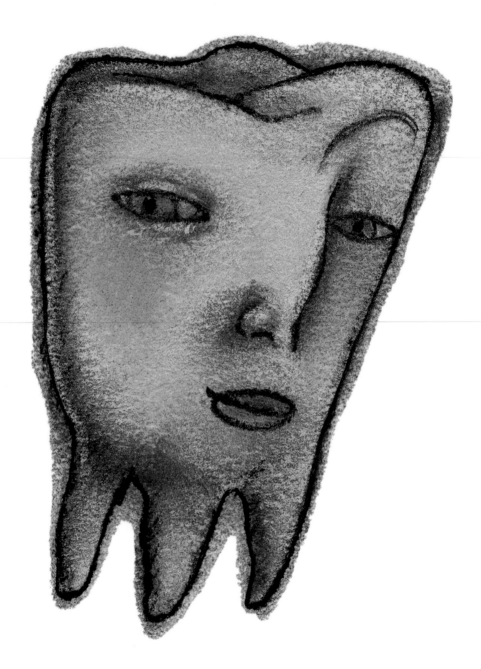

A person's teeth are also affected by an eating disorder.

Someone battling an eating disorder may feel overwhelmed with anxiety.

I still couldn't quit, even knowing how much bulimia was harming me. Eventually, I got a tear in my esophagus from throwing up. That was pretty serious. They rushed me to the hospital and there was surgery and recovery and—I'll just say it was a really rough time, okay?

I had to drop out of school, of course. I was pretty much a wreck at that point. My parents were really there for me, though, and when I recovered from the surgery, they brought me here to the clinic where I now work part-time, though of course I was a patient, then, and a pretty sick one, too.

One of the first things the doctors here did was to put me on medication called amitriptyline—also called Elavil—for the anxiety. Amitriptyline is what's called a tricyclic antidepressant, and it's used both for anxiety and for bulimia. It's not for everybody, because it can cause some heart problems and has some other side effects, but it really helped me to get the anxiety issue under control so I could face the bulimia.

I stayed on the drug and had therapy for about eight months, then I went off the drug and had more therapy for almost a year longer. It was really hard work, but it was all worth it, Lindsay. I haven't binged or purged in two years now, and I've learned some positive, healthy ways to deal with the bad feelings, the feelings I was trying to run away from before. And one of the best things is that I'm starting to help other people. Because of what I went through, I can talk to people with eating disorders and really connect with them. I'm planning to get a degree in nutrition so that I can learn even more about this whole area. I feel as though I got my life back, if that makes any sense.

And I hope the same thing will happen for Maria. You said they put her on Prozac, right? That's actually one of the main medications

When treatment is successful, a person who once suffered from an eating disorder will be able to enjoy normal, healthy eating habits.

Medication often has a role to play in the successful treatment of eating disorders.

they use for bulimia. It belongs to a group of drugs called selective serotonin reuptake inhibitors, a lot of big words that just mean they make more serotonin available in your brain. Serotonin is a chemical that's important for regulating your moods and your desire to eat, among many, many other things.

This is so long, it's turning into a book, Lindsay. I know I need to sign off, but before I do, would you just let me say a few more things to you, girlfriend? Eating disorders are nothing to mess around with. I know it makes you angry when I ask you to talk to someone about what you're going through, but I'm going to risk getting you angry again, because I care about you. You've seen two examples now of how awful life can get when an eating problem gets out of hand: Maria and me. We both ended up in the hospital with life-threatening emergencies. You may not be as bad off as we were, but please don't wait until you get worse to ask for help.

Depression is also a serious problem. I certainly don't think I can tell you that you're depressed just from our e-mails, Lindsay, but I'm thinking I see some hints in many of the things you wrote, especially in this last e-mail. Depression can play a big part in eating disorders. Sometimes just talking it out with a counselor or a therapist can help a person deal with depression. If that alone doesn't help, some of the same medications used to treat anxiety disorders and bulimia can also help with depression.

Okay, that's enough advice for now (or maybe more than enough, hmm?).

Thanks for listening to me,
Gina

P.S. I forgot to mention this, but it's important: those pro-ana websites can be really negative places to visit, Lindsay. They can trigger dangerous thoughts and emotions in people who have eating disorders or who are recovering from one. Remember the website where you found my posts? That's a really positive site, dedicated to helping people get better.

The FDA bases its approval on specific research results. Sometimes, a particular use for a drug may have been thoroughly researched by many studies, while other uses lack the same amount of research. In that case, the drug label will only include the uses that have met the FDA's stringent research requirements. Physicians, however, may continue to prescribe that drug for other "off-label" uses.

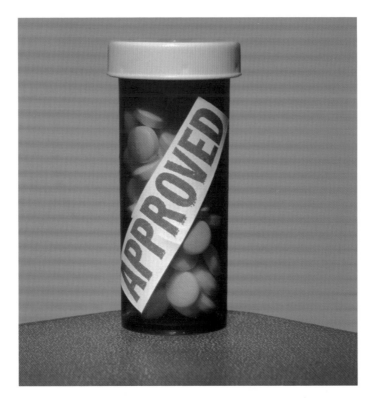

Each drug must pass the FDA's stringent requirements before it can be officially approved. Medical practitioners, however, may use the drug for "off-label" perscriptions.

Treatment For Eating Disorders

There are still many questions about how to deal with eating disorders. Present-day treatment for eating disorders—whether it is provided from a relatively inexpensive community health center on an outpatient basis or at a more expensive inpatient facility—falls into three categories: medical, behavioral, and pharmacological.

Medical Therapy

Many medical treatments have been tried in the history of treating eating disorders. These treatments include nutritional counseling, vitamins, thyroid extract, calf pituitary, insulin, testosterone, L-dopa, prefrontal lobotomy, antidepressants, and electroconvulsive therapy.

Behavioral Therapy

According to several studies, both cognitive-behavioral therapy (CBT) and psychiatric drug treatment can be effective in the treatment of bulimia. When used alone, CBT is more effective than medication used alone. Most effective of all is treatment that combines both. For more information on CBT, see chapter 5.

Pharmacological Therapy

This treatment includes the use of the psychiatric drugs named and described

pituitary: A small organ attached to the brain that produces internal secretions that either directly or indirectly affect most of the basic body functions.

insulin: A hormone produced by the pancreas that is necessary for the metabolism of carbohydrates.

testosterone: A hormone produced by the testes that is responsible for the development of male secondary sex characteristics.

L-dopa: A drug used to treat Parkinson's disease.

prefrontal lobotomy: The surgical removal of the prefrontal part of the brain.

throughout this book as being effective in the treatment of eating disorders.

The Interdisciplinary Treatment Team

According to psychiatric experts, an interdisciplinary team is required for the proper care of patients with eating disorders. The American Dietetic Association (ADA) views eating disorders as "psychiatric disorder(s) with major medical complications," and takes the position that "psychiatric management is the foundation of treatment and should be instituted for all patients in combination with other treatment modalities." The ADA recommends the following individuals be included on the interdisciplinary team:

- A physician or advanced practice nurse who is familiar with eating disorders to perform physical and dental exams, manage medication, and monitor the medical condition.
- A credentialed clinician who is experienced in eating disorders to provide psychotherapy.
- Nurses to monitor the patient's status in inpatient and partial hospitalization settings.
- Recreation and occupational therapists to help the patient acquire healthy daily living and recreational skills.
- A registered dietician to assess the nutritional status, knowledge

electroconvulsive therapy: The use of electric current and drugs to induce seizures. Often used in treating depression.

cognitive-behavioral therapy: Treatment that alters maladaptive thoughts and behaviors, using learning principles.

A Case Study

A fifteen-year-old female named Betty was brought to the clinic by her mother, who suspected that her daughter was bulimic. A year earlier, Betty had been raped while walking home from a dance at her school. After the clinician completed Betty's evaluation, a diagnosis was made: Betty had post-traumatic stress disorder. She was experiencing flashbacks from her trauma—and these flashbacks would trigger her episodes of purging. She reported felling a sense of relief from purging, an escape from the thoughts that haunted her. Betty explained that when she was purging, that was all she could think about; purging might not be pleasant, but it was a relief from the terrible memories that plagued her. The clinician treated Betty with medication for her anxiety and referred her to a psychologist for counseling. As Betty experienced relief from her post-traumatic stress, her bulimia symptoms disappeared as well.

base, motivation, and current eating and behavioral status; to develop the nutrition segment of the treatment plan; to implement the treatment plan, and to support the patient in accomplishing the goals of the plan.

Eating Disorders and Other Psychiatric Disorders

There is a high frequency of correlation between bulimia nervosa and other anxiety and substance-related disorders. Abuse of alcohol and stimulants occurs in a third of individuals with bulimia nervosa. According to one researcher, between two and 50 percent of women with bulimia nervosa have some type of personality disorder; borderline, antisocial, histrionic or narcissistic personality disorders are most common.

Because of this correlation, it is often necessary for both or all psychiatric disorders present to be treated in a patient with eating disorders. For example, a patient who suffers from both bulimia and depression may need to be treated with psychiatric drugs and behavioral therapy for both her depression and her bulimia. (For more information on the treatment of anxiety disorders, which often co-exist with eating disorders, see *Drug Therapy and Anxiety Disorders*, another volume in this series.)

> correlation: When two conditions occur at the same time.

Psychiatric drugs are powerful chemicals with risks and side effects.

Chapter Five

Risks and Side Effects

Date: January 13
Subject: Update on Lindsay
From: Lindsay<lgirl@compnet.com>
To: <Happywithme@college.edu>

Dear Gina,

This is Lindsay's mother writing. Lindsay asked me to get in touch with you and let you know what happened this past week.

I've been terribly worried about her for the past few months. She had lost so much weight that she looked absolutely emaciated. She became furious when I tried to talk to her about it, however, and absolutely refused to go back to one of the doctors here in town who specializes in eating disorders. She kept insisting she was fine and that she wasn't losing any more weight. And she always wore baggy clothes that covered everything but her face, so I couldn't be absolutely sure. I made her get on our bathroom scale once every week, and according to the scale, she was right—she wasn't losing at all. I was very confused, because she just kept looking worse and worse as the weeks went by. I even went to my doctor's office and had them weigh me, then came home and got on our scale to make sure it was correct.

Last Friday, they weighed Lindsay at school and the nurse called me immediately. I was horrified when she told me Lindsay's weight—twelve pounds less than what our scale said. It turns out that Lindsay had learned from one of the pro-anorexia websites to hide weights in her clothes when I made her weigh herself here. At school, the nurse had also been getting more and more concerned about how she looked, and when she asked Lindsay to get on the scale, Lindsay's weights were here at home.

I felt incredibly stupid about all of this. I kept depending on that number on the scale when I should have trusted my own judgment about how she looked.

When I admitted her to the eating disorders clinic, she was furious at me, but I didn't feel I had any choice. The funny thing is, I also had the sensation that she was at least a little bit relieved that I forced her to get help.

For the first two weeks, Lindsay isn't allowed to e-mail or phone anyone, and only her father and I can visit her. If she gains enough weight to meet the goals they set for her, she'll earn more privileges as far as contacting friends. They'll be supervising her time online, though, and I'm glad for that. I think the pro-anorexia sites were very damaging to her.

With Lindsay's permission, I read some of your e-mails to her, Gina, and I appreciate so much the way you've tried to help her. I hope you won't think I've invaded your privacy, but as I told Lindsay, I needed to know you had her best interests at heart before I could agree to contact you.

Family members can provide important support to an individual being treated for an eating disorder. Love and acceptance play an essential role in the individual's road to recovery.

I see from your emails that you also have been through some difficult times, so I know you'll understand when I tell you that the therapist has diagnosed Lindsay as being depressed. He hopes to start her on a medication that will help her with the depression. He tells me that there is no medication that can "cure" the anorexia, but that treating the depression is an important step in helping her get well. The treatment team is to decide today which psychiatric drug to use, since they want to make sure to use the one with the least side effects.

I'll be glad to pass along messages to Lindsay if you answer this. Thanks again for all the help and encouragement you've given to her.

Sincerely,
Carole

Some people think that psychiatric drugs are dangerous substances to be avoided at all costs—while other people see these medications as easy answers to many of life's problems. Neither viewpoint is accurate.

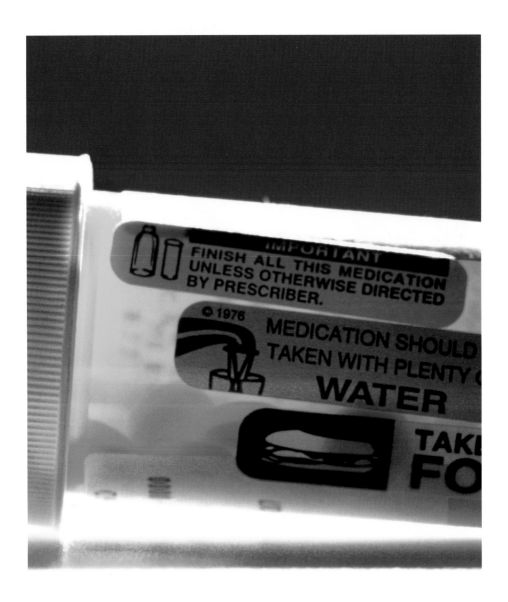

The risks of a particular drug may be increased if the patient does not exactly follow medication instructions.

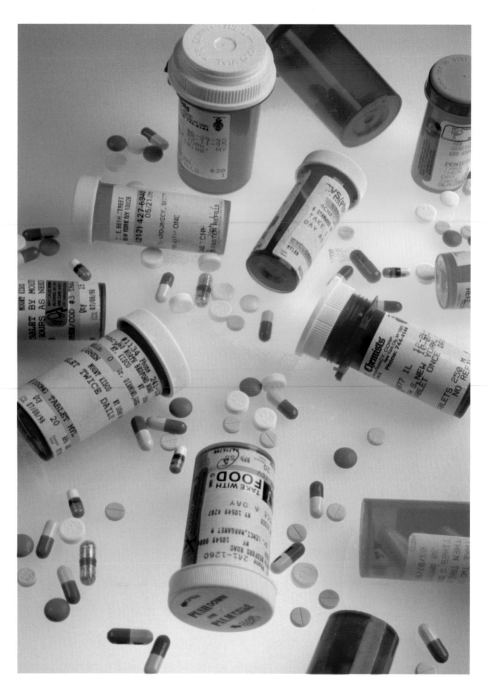

It is important to let your medical practitioner know about all medications you are already taking. Drug interactions can be dangerous.

Date: January 14
Subject: RE: Update on Lindsay
From: <Happywithme@college.edu>
To: Lindsay<lgirl@compnet.com>

Dear Carole,

I really appreciate your letting me know about Lindsay's situation. I can only imagine how difficult this must be for you.

Patients who are absolutely determined to go on with their anorexia sometimes learn many "tricks" like the one with the weights that Lindsay used. You couldn't have known—I mean, who would ever dream a person would do that?

Please let Lindsay know that I am very interested in her progress and that I will continue to hope for the best for her.

I'll hope for the same for you, too, Carole. I'm so glad that Lindsay has your love and determination to help her through this. My own parents provided that kind of support for me, and I will always be grateful!

I'm glad that Lindsay will be taking psychiatric drugs as part of her recovery. I know from personal experience that these can be a big help. The human body is very complicated, though, and chemicals can sometimes have unforeseen results. You and Lindsay need to work with the doctors carefully to monitor the side effects of her drug therapy.

Best,
Gina

epilepsy: A disease caused by recurrent seizures.

glaucoma: A group of eye diseases caused by the build up of pressure within the eye.

hyperthyroidism: A disease caused by an excessive amount of thyroid hormone.

prostatic hypertrophy: Excessive growth of the prostate gland.

urinary retention: The inability to completely empty the bladder.

All drugs have the potential to interact with other drugs, sometimes causing dangerous and even deadly reactions, so all medications should be taken under the care of a physician. The various classes of drugs used to treat eating disorders each have their own side effects.

Tricyclic Antidepressants [TCAs]

TCAs should not be used by people who have an abnormal heart rhythm or who have recently had a heart attack. These drugs can make an abnormal heart rhythm worse and may dangerously affect the function of the heart. Individuals who want to use TCAs must use extra caution if they have: bipolar disorder, epilepsy, glaucoma, low blood pressure, psychotic disorders, hyperthyroidism, prostatic hypertrophy, or urinary retention. Alcohol should not be used with TCAs, nor should they be given to patients who are high-risk for suicide.

TCAs can cause drowsiness, dizziness, blurry vision, constipation, dry mouth, fatigue, increased heart rate, low blood pressure,

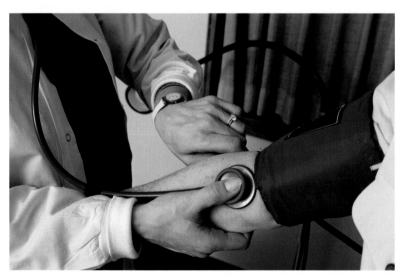

Blood pressure should be monitored when a person is taking a TCA or MAOI.

The first best-selling book on weight control in America was published in 1918. *Diet and Health with a Key to the Calories* was written by Lulu Hunt Peters, who said: "How anyone can want to be anything but thin is beyond my intelligence." In the wake of World War I, when food shortages were common, Peters wrote, "There are hundreds of thousands of individuals all over America who are hoarding food. They have vast amounts of this valuable commodity stored away in their own anatomy."

Peters was an enthusiastic proponent of the new system of counting calories, and wrote that women "should know and also use the word calorie as frequently, or more frequently, than you use the words foot, yard, quart, gallon and so forth.

. . . Hereafter you are going to eat calories of food. Instead of saying one slice of bread, or a piece of pie, you will say 100 calories of bread, 350 calories of pie."

Adapted from *Fasting Girls: The Emergence of Anorexia Nervosa as a Modern Disease*, by Joan Jacobs Brumberg.

agitation, sweating, weight gain. Less commonly, they have been known to cause insomnia, sexual dysfunction, and urinary difficulty.

Monoamine Oxidase Inhibitors

These medications are rarely prescribed for eating disorders, because they entail many risks and dietary restrictions. MAOIs can cause a stroke if taken with adrenaline or adrenaline-like substances. This means that individuals who use MAOIs must also follow a very strict diet that avoids both medicines and foods containing such substances, including (this is not an exhaustive list): several cough and cold medicines, aged or fermented foods, all cheese or foods that contain cheese (except for cottage cheese and cream cheese), cream, sour cream, yogurt, foods fermented with yeast, brewer's yeast, liver, bologna, corned beef, hot dogs, liverwurst, pepperoni, salami, sausage, fava beans, sauerkraut, pickles, soy sauce, licorice, caviar, anchovies, dried fruits such as raisins, prunes, and figs, raspberries, chocolate, bananas, pickled herring, and drinks that contain caffeine, although a few may be allowed. These drugs may also cause weight gain, dry mouth, insomnia, impaired sexual response, and light-headedness because of low blood pressure.

pheochromocytoma: A tumor that is usually accompanied by high blood pressure.

Individuals with the following conditions should not take MAOIs: congestive heart failure, high blood pressure, liver disease, or pheochromocytoma. Those with bipolar disorder, epilepsy, low blood pressure, or a psychotic disorder should exercise extra caution in using MAOIs. Side effects for these individuals can include agitation, constipation, dizziness, headaches, insomnia, sedation, sexual

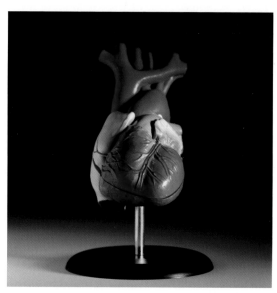

MAOIs can affect heart function.

Careful monitoring from a medical practitioner decreases the risks posed by psychiatric medications.

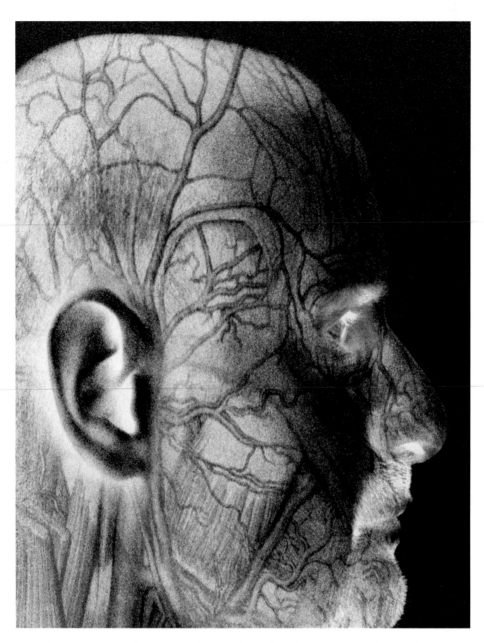

The human mind is complicated and delicate—and psychiatric drugs can affect it in powerful ways. For instance, SSRIs can be effective and beneficial, but serotonin syndrome, a dangerous possible side effect of combining SSRIs with other drugs, includes potentially fatal reactions.

When a drug is sold in the United States, the FDA requires the manufacturer to provide a complete written report on the drug: what the drug is made of; how the drug is to be used; how much of the drug to prescribe; what other foods or drugs to avoid while taking this drug; possible side effects or dangers associated with the drug; what the drug comes in (pill? liquid? capsule?); and for whom the drug should be prescribed. All of this information is contained in the package insert, which drug manufacturers are required to enclose in every medication package sold in the United States. Doctors can obtain the same information from a reference book called *The Physicians' Desk Reference* (PDR).

dysfunction, tremor, muscle twitching, and weight gain. MAOIs have the potential to cause a hypertensive crisis, in which dangerously high blood pressure increases the risk of a stroke, brain damage, or death. It is important to consult with the prescribing physician and learn from her all the other medications (both prescription and nonprescription) and recreational drug compounds that must be avoided.

Selective Serotonin Reuptake Inhibitors

SSRIs must be used with great caution by people who have bipolar disorder, diabetes, epilepsy, kidney problems, or a psychotic disorder. If patients take more than one SSRI, or a combination of an SSRI and an MAOI, Saint-John's-wort, or trytophan, they could experience the serotonin syndrome, which includes potentially fatal changes in blood pressure and pulse, mental status, and

A psychiatric medication is never a magic pill. Its side effects should always be carefully monitored by a medical practitioner.

hyperactivity. Other side effects may include fatigue, nausea, diarrhea, vomiting, dry mouth, dizziness, visual disturbances, weakness, sweating, decreased appetite, rash, sexual dysfunction, agitation, insomnia, anxiety, and tremor.

Psychiatric drugs can have powerful effects on the human body. Some of these are beneficial and healing, but other effects may be harmful and destructive. The benefits should always outweigh the risks—and even then, individuals taking these drugs should work closely with their physicians or psychiatrists to monitor their bodies' responses to the medication.

Alternative and supplementary treatments may include special diets.

Chapter Six

Alternative and Supplementary Treatments

Date: March 20
Subject: I'm Back
From: Lindsay<lgirl@compnet.com>
To: <Happywithme@college.edu>

Dear Gina,

Finally! I get to write my own e-mail messages again! The doctors said I could have died because my weight went so low, so they told me about all these privileges, like e-mail, that I could earn back when I gained the first ten pounds. I think they were just doing anything they could to get me to gain some weight. (Just between you and me, Gina, I didn't think I would ever, ever be happy about gaining weight, but I actually feel pretty good. It's like I'm thinking differently about a lot of things now.)

The first month I was here at the clinic was awful. Even the thought of gaining back a single pound made me frantic, and then I got more depressed than ever. That's why I didn't answer most of your messages—sorry. This second month has been a lot better, though, now that I've had two months of therapy and the sertraline (Zoloft) is working on the depression. I don't think I had any idea how depressed I was, or how long I'd been that way. The therapist thinks that it's probably been going on ever since my parents got divorced. Funny—both my parents got counseling back then, especially my mom, but nobody paid much attention to how I was doing.

Anyway, I still have a long way to go. I know that. But in the last few weeks, I've started to care about whether I get well or not. Maria sent me some messages through my dad (I'm speaking to him again, most of the time) that first month, but then she had a relapse and started purging and all that. She's having outpatient treatment, so she has to check in with the people at the hospital every day and tell them what she ate and all.

She has to keep a food journal, which is the same thing they're making me do. I have to write down everything I eat or drink all day long—and I'm eating a lot, let me tell you—and how I felt when I ate it.

Here's a list of what they want me to eat in one day (with nothing in it that's low-fat!), so you can be as amazed as I am:

Breakfast: cereal with milk; two pieces of toast with butter and jelly; eggs with bacon or sausage; and orange juice

Lunch: meat, vegetables, potatoes, and dessert

Dinner: the same kind of meal as lunch

Learning to eat the daily requirement of vegetables may be a challenge for someone struggling with an eating disorder.

Do you ever feel like everything in your life is out of control? We all feel this way sometimes, but people with an eating disorder may have this feeling more than the rest of us. They often feel like eating is the only thing they can control. In a life that demands too much from them, they can decide how much food they put in their mouths. Not eating makes them feel empowered, as though they have gained some control of their life. Ultimately, of course, this sense of control is destructive; it traps them in a lifestyle that limits them physically and emotionally.

I have to have snacks mid-morning, mid-afternoon, and bedtime, too! At first, I couldn't even imagine eating all that, but now it's not so bad.

Gina, I want to say thanks for all the help you've been to me. You were right all along, you know, about thinking I had anorexia. I'm sorry again that I was sometimes rude to you in my emails. I was terrified that if I gave in and agreed with you for even a moment, I'd lose control and end up in a place like this. But now, here I am, and I think it's going to save my life.

Write to me soon and let me know how you're doing, okay?

Best always,
Lindsay

P.S. Oh, and guess what, Gina? There are actually some guys here! I never expected that, but it turns out you were right about that 10 percent. One of them is kind of cool, a guy named Jason. We spend a lot of time just talking, you know, about how we got here and what we plan to do when we're better.

Taking part in a support group or talking with a counselor can provide vital help to someone battling an eating disorder.

P.P.S. The medication is a big help, just like you said it would be. I don't really like to think about putting all those chemicals in my body for very long, though. The doctor has been telling my mom and me about some other alternative treatments that might help too.

Cognitive-Behavioral Therapy

Several different studies have shown that both psychiatric drugs and CBT can help in the treatment of bulimia nervosa. Used alone, CBT, which is a treatment that helps patients alter their maladaptive thoughts and behaviors by using techniques that come from social learning theory and behaviorism, is more effective than medication used alone. Combining the two treatments has proven to be the most effective treatment of all. CBT usually lasts for a period of approximately six months and has resulted in significant reductions of binge eating and/or purging.

social learning theory: A theory that emphasizes the interaction of environmental variables and the process of knowing.

cognitive: The process of knowing, including perception, memory, and judgment.

CBT addresses the cognitive aspects of bulimia nervosa. These aspects include the patient's preoccupation with body, food, weight, and perfectionism. Many health care professionals who deal with eating problems stress that the common element in all of these disorders is the presence of low self-esteem; this aspect is also addressed in CBT.

The cognitive-behavioral therapist also works with patients on the behavioral components of their disorder, including dieting and eating habits, binge eating, purging, and disturbed eating habits. The first goal of CBT is to help individuals with eating disorders gain

The goal for a person with an eating disorder is to help her reach the point where she can once more enjoy food in a healthy and beneficial manner.

If a patient has medical complications (an esophageal tear, electrolyte disturbance, or heart arrhythmia, for instance), inpatient treatment may be essential. Inpatient treatment may also help the patient break the cycle of destructive eating habits and learn coping strategies, such as relaxation techniques, how to tolerate the feeling of fullness, and how to keep food down. Unfortunately, there is a lack of good inpatient programs. Many insurance plans will not pay for inpatient treatment, so the cost of this treatment may also be an obstacle in many cases.

control over their food intake. Because bingeing sometimes begins as a reaction to calorie-restricted diets, such restrictions are avoided. Instead, the patient is taught to record both the food they eat and the feelings they experience at the time. The therapist provides feedback on nutritional balance, the triggers for disordered eating symptoms, and other aspects of the patient's recorded behavior. Patients are instructed in cognitive methods for challenging rigid thought patterns, methods for improving self-esteem, assertiveness training, and the identification and appropriate expression of feelings.

Anorexia nervosa, which seldom responds to psychiatric medications alone, is most effectively treated by intensive psychodynamic psychotherapy. This therapy helps patients integrate their feelings about their bodies, their lives, and the outside world. It teaches them positive ways to gain control over their lives.

A healthy diet is an essential part of emotional and physical well-being.

Anorexia and other eating disorders are particularly common among adolescent girls who may see controlling their weight as a way to achieve perfection.

Homeopathic Treatment for Eating Disorders

Homeopathy is a form of alternative medicine that treats disease and disorders from a very different perspective than conventional medicine. It looks at a person's entire physical and mental being rather than dividing a patient into various symptoms and disorders. Homeopathic medicine uses tiny doses to stimulate the body's ability to heal itself. In some cases, these doses may be administered only once every few months or years.

According to Judyth Reichenberg-Ullman and Robert Ullman, authors of *Prozac Free: Homeopathic Medicine for Depression, Anxiety, and Other Mental and Emotional Problems*, homeopathy offers safe, natural alternatives that can supplement or replace conventional pharmaceutical treatment. They recommend this form of treatment because it has fewer side effects than conventional drugs.

Hospitalization Versus Outpatient Therapy

Because of the current high costs of inpatient medical care, fewer patients with eating disorders are hospitalized today, so both bulimia nervosa and anorexia nervosa are now being treated more frequently on an outpatient basis. Outpatient therapy has proven to be useful, both on an individual and group basis, but the outcome depends on the stage of the disease. (If a patient's body weight drops too low, however, hospitalization for nutritional rehabilitation may become necessary.)

Other Alternative Treatments

There are other alternative options for patients who want to try supplementing therapy and drug treatment. Few studies verify their effectiveness, but some people who suffer from eating disorders have successful encounters with alternative therapies.

One option is acupuncture, a form of traditional Chinese medicine. Thin needles are inserted into pressure points, influencing the flow of energy through the body. Acupuncture is often used to treat depression and anxiety, both of which accompany eating disorders. Today, it is being used specifically to treat anorexia and bulimia in certain clinics and programs. One German study focused on the role of acupuncture in increasing the levels of leptin in the body, a hormone that regulate metabolism, and found that people with anorexia have lower levels of leptin. A Chinese study of acupuncture in turn found that it could increase levels of leptin in anorexia patients. There's still much more to be found out about the possible use of acupuncture in treating eating disorders.

Art therapy is another option that can be beneficial to many people suffering from an eating disorder. For some people, anorexia, bulimia, or another eating disorder is a way to cope with a traumatic experience or loss of control in life, although it may be unconscious. Art, either done on one's own or in a guide art therapy program, can offer a different outlet of expression. The art produced can be in any form, from drawing and painting to photography or video production.

Some patients undergo Eye Movement Desensitization and Reprocessing (EMDR), involving a series of specific eye movements while remembering a traumatic past event. The eye movements help patients cope with traumatic memories, and to process them in the present day. EMDR is generally used to treat people with Post-Traumatic Stress Disorder, but can also be useful for those suffering from an eating disorder stemming from an event in the past, such as sexual assault. Many studies support the efficacy of EMDR, though other researchers dispute its use.

Many inpatient medical care centers offer these and other alternative treatments. Sometimes patients respond better to an alternative form of therapy, in conjunction with medical treatment and more tradition forms of therapy. It is up to the patient and her or his medical team to decide with treatment options are right.

Further Reading

Brumberg, Joan Jacobs. *Fasting Girls, The Emergence of Anorexia Nervosa as a Modern Disease.* New York: Random Books, 2000.

Cutts, Shannon. *Beating Ana: How to Outsmart Your Eating Disorder and Take Your Life Back*. Deerfeild Beach, Flor.: Health Communications, Inc., 2009.

Danowski, Debbie, and Pedro Lazaro. *Why Can't I Stop Eating?* Center City, Minn.: Hazelden, 2000.

Drummond, Edward. *The Complete Guide to Psychiatric Drugs.* New York: John Wiley & Sons, 2006.

Gorman, Jack M. *The Essential Guide to Psychiatric Drugs.* New York: St. Martin's Press, 2007.

Hall, Lindsey and Leigh Cohn. *Bulimia, a Guide to Recovery.* Carlsbad, Calif.: Gurze Books, 2011.

Pettit, Christine. *Starving: A Personal Journey through Anorexia.* Ada, Mich.: Fleming H. Revell Company, 2003.

For More Information

American Psychological Association
www.apa.org

American Psychiatric Association
www.psych.org

Eating Disorders in a Disordered Culture
www.eating.ucdavis.edu

National Eating Disorders Association
www.edap.org

National Mental Health Association
www.nmha.org

Publisher's Note:
The websites listed on this page were active at the time of publication. The publisher is not responsible for websites that have changed their address or discontinued operation since the date of publication. The publisher will review and update the websites upon each reprint.

Index

About the Author & Consultants

Shirley Brinkerhoff was a writer, editor, speaker, and musician. She published six young adult novels, six informational books for young people, scores of short stories and articles, and taught at writers' conferences throughout the United States.

Mary Ann McDonnell, Ph.D., R.N., is the owner of South Shore Psychiatric Services, where she provides psychiatric services to children and adolescents. She has worked as a psychiatric nurse at Franciscan Hospital for Children and has been a clinical instructor for Northeastern University and Boston College advanced-practice nursing students. She was also the director of clinical trials in the pediatric psychopharmacology research unit at Massachusetts General Hospital. Her areas of expertise are bipolar disorder in children and adolescents, ADHD, and depression.

Donald Esherick has worked in regulatory affairs at Rhone-Poulenc Rorer, Wyeth Pharmaceuticals, Pfizer, and Pharmalink Consulting. He specializes in the chemistry section (manufacture and testing) of investigational and marketed drugs.